LEGGINGS ARE
NOT PANTS

LEGGINGS ARE NOT PANTS

... AND OTHER FALSEHOODS

JEANETTE KEENE

NEW DEGREE PRESS

COPYRIGHT © 2018 JEANETTE KEENE

LEGGINGS ARE NOT PANTS

... and other falsehoods

ISBN   978-1-64137-186-5   *Paperback*

          978-1-64137-187-2   *Ebook*

To all of the past, present, and future women who heard "no"
in the pursuit of a goal and persisted anyway, thank you.

CONTENTS

INTRODUCTION   9

FALSEHOOD 1. ATHLEISURE IS JUST A TREND   25

FALSEHOOD 2. ATHLEISURE STARTED AS FASHION   39

FALSEHOOD 3. ATHLEISURE IS EASY TO DEFINE   59

FALSEHOOD 4. ATHLEISURE IS BRAND DRIVEN   79

FALSEHOOD 5. ONE SIZE FITS ALL   99

FALSEHOOD 6. LEGGINGS ARE NOT PANTS   117

FALSEHOOD 7. ATHLEISURE IS LAZY   131

FALSEHOOD 8. "SHRINK IT AND PINK IT" WORKS   151

FALSEHOOD 9. MEN SHOULD DESIGN WOMEN'S CLOTHES   175

FALSEHOOD 10. ATHLEISURE IS SUSTAINABLE   197

FALSEHOOD 11. ATHLEISURE HAS LIMITED INFLUENCE   219

              FALSEHOOD SUMMARIES & CONCLUSION   237

              ACKNOWLEDGEMENTS   251

              REFERENCES CITED   253

INTRODUCTION

———

"Athleisure is a fashion trend and is subjective. The popularity of athleisure could change if a fashion magazine or top designers that dictate fashion decide something else is now trendy and acceptable to wear."

This particular quote is from a conversation I had with someone in the apparel industry regarding the popularity of athleisure among women. While top designers and fashion magazines may have greatly influenced what women wear at one point, those days have passed. Increasingly, women are driving the narrative around what they want to wear and who influences them.

Do you agree with this person's assessment? Not only do I not agree with this statement, I believe this way of thinking is as passé as the thought that if a brand wants to sell women a product all they need to do is make it pink (we'll get into this in a later chapter). This statement is just the first of many "falsehoods" that I aim to disprove throughout this book in regard to modern women, how they are choosing to dress and why.

By the way, I'll get more into what athleisure is and how it came about in the next chapter but for now if you don't know what athleisure is, it's the word used to describe when athletic clothes, or activewear, are worn in a leisure setting. For instance, when women wear leggings and a hoodie to the grocery store instead of the gym.

What this person and others who agree with the opening statement fail to understand is that athleisure is not *just* a trend, its popularity evolved into a change in the way women are approaching the clothes they choose to buy and wear. What started out as a few women wearing yoga pants beyond the yoga studio exploded into a conscious decision to wear clothes that are as comfortable as they are stylish *and* work with their increasingly demanding lifestyles.

Even though the number of women that participated in sports and athletic activities continued to grow over the past few decades, women's activewear (another term for athletic clothes) and footwear remained an afterthought to men's. Underserved in the athletic market for years, women flocked to new activewear options that were also stylish, proudly wearing the clothes both at the yoga studio and on the street.

The more other women saw these women wearing their athletic clothes out in public, the more other women purchased and wore it in a similar way. Before long the act of wearing athletic clothing in a leisure way was so popular the name athleisure was used to identify the *phenomenon*.

The fashion industry did not dictate this as a trend but after seeing that women weren't going to stop wearing it, top designers, brands, and retailers got on board and started offering women their own version of athleisure and activewear. What started out in the 2000s as women deciding to wear yoga pants beyond the studio impacted not only the athletic apparel industry but also the fashion industry altogether.

You know that athletic clothing and footwear are undeniably fashionable when Anna Wintour, *Vogue* editor-in-chief and creative director for Conde Nast collaborated with Nike in 2018 around two pairs of women's Air Jordan sneakers.

Offered in red and white leather, Wintour's signature "AWOK" acronym (Anna Wintour OK) used to sign off on her magazine pages was added to the soles of the shoes. To promote the sneakers, Anna appears in an ad wearing a pair of the sneakers at her desk while sinking shots in her office basketball hoop.

In 2015, the U.S. athleisure market was worth $44 billion. Activewear sales grew 16 percent while non-activewear sales only grew 2 percent, showing not only the popularity of these clothes but also a shift in purchases towards athletic clothing.[1]

Top brands offering clothes that could be worn as athleisure saw significant sales gains. The company that helped start the trend, Lululemon, doubled sales between 2010 and 2016, growing an additional 12.5 percent in 2017 with continued growth expected throughout 2018. Similarly, between 2010 and 2016, Under Armour sales tripled while Nike, adidas, and Puma sales each increased double-digits.[2]

Collectively, between 2011 and 2016, the athletic gear market grew almost seven times as fast as the overall apparel market to become a third of the entire clothing market.[3] That growth

---

1   ("Is Activewear Industry Finally Becoming Overstretched?" 2016)
2   (Kell 2016)
3   (Hanbury 2018)

doesn't even include all of the non-athletic brands and retailers that launched their own activewear and athleisure lines and collaborations to get in on the action as well.

That kind of growth shows that athleisure became more than just a trend, it helped spark a fashion movement. More women realized that functional and stylish clothes that allowed them not only to crush their gym workouts but also weekend errands or work days by being able to head from an event to the gym without missing a beat was what they wanted.

The way athleisure bubbled up, or trickled up, from the streets to become mainstream is not a new concept. Past trends have given way to popular clothing gems such as goth, hippie dress, baggy jeans, ripped jeans, and motorcycle leather jackets to name a few.

What differentiates the popularity of athleisure from other trends that have faded is the shift in mindset and lasting impact. Athleisure isn't going to be replaced by another trend, it's evolving the way women dress and their influence on fashion similar to other changes of the past, including when women began wearing pants.

Despite articles proclaiming the slowdown and end of athleisure, women kept buying it and wearing it. Despite backlash around women wearing leggings, women kept wearing them. Despite limited activewear options for the average woman, women found a way to create more options and expand the athleisure options available to more women.

As more athleisure options were offered, women didn't have to choose between comfort and style, they learned both were possible...in the same garment. And once women realized they could have both, the same requirements became necessary for other parts of their wardrobe.

This shift is more than women wanting to add pockets to their skirts or wear leggings to brunch, this is about women demanding clothes that meet the needs of their modern life in every respect – work, play, ease, comfort, and more. Instead of clothing trends being dictated to women, women are now taking a more active role in creating clothing trends.

This is relevant because women's apparel has either been dictated by the fashion industry largely run by men or ignored by the sports apparel industry that has also been run by men. But that is changing. Women are more vocal than ever about what kind of clothes they want both literally and through the purchases they are making.

As athleisure rose in popularity, other clothes were impacted. Leggings sales skyrocketed while denim sales declined because enough women decided that leggings were now the bottom garment de jour. Similarly, sneakers are increasingly replacing high heels, not just at the office but on the runway as well.

And if brands won't make what women want, they are willing to create it themselves. From Tyler Haney, the founder of Outdoor Voices to Polina Veksler and Alex Waldman, the co-founders of Universal Standard, women are changing the clothing options available and the way the apparel industry works. Whether the ripple effect of the past several years has distanced itself from the shift change enough to be visible to everyone or not, the future of women's fashion will be dictated by women—founders, leaders, designers, and customers.

Most importantly, the popularity and wide spread adoption of athleisure has prompted discussions around inclusivity, body shape acceptance, gender product assumptions, and even sustainability. Authenticity is increasingly important across both messaging and product offering. Female communities praise brands that do this well, leaving others that do not connect with what is important to them behind.

Let's not get it twisted. I'm not saying that all women live their lives in leggings and sweatshirts all day. What I hope you'll take away from this book is that athleisure helped to spark a change in how more women approach their clothes and wardrobe through the benefits they discovered in wearing it. Moreover, the popularity of athleisure itself sparked discussions around what is considered appropriate dress that women continue to challenge.

For instance, why can't business attire have more stretch, offer pockets, and be made with moisture-wicking fabric? Similarly, why can't sneakers be considered appropriate business dress for women? Increasingly, women are taking a more active role in pushing expectations around dress codes, redefining what is considered appropriate dress versus what they have been told they are *supposed* to wear and when.

And, as more women rise into leadership positions, official dress codes may be revised even further. Is it only a matter of time before a Silicon Valley female founder graces the cover of *Fast Company* in her own version of a t-shirt, jeans, and sneaker uniform that is already popular among male founders? I think so.

**

So, who am I and why do I care about all of this? I've always had a strong interest in fashion as well as participated in some form of physical activity or sport throughout my life. I studied fashion merchandising in college and grad school as well as worked in various roles within the retail and wholesale industries from research and product development to marketing and merchandising.

As someone who has maintained a regular workout regimen but was frustrated with the workout clothing options, I was very excited when fashionable activewear became available. I paid attention to the new brands and clothes, not only as a customer but also as someone who was used to focusing on clothing trends as a part of my job.

I grew up a competitive gymnast and dancer who practically lived in leotards, sweatshirts, leggings, tracksuits, and other athletic and comfortable clothes throughout my life. When given the choice between comfort and fashion, I usually chose the more comfortable option. "You're going to wear that?!?" was a phrase I got used to hearing.

In high school I began exploring how to exercise and stay fit beyond the dance studio. By the time I graduated I'd learned how to lift weights from my father and how to snag a cardio machine before peak hours. Over the years, I've continued to try different ways to exercise as part of my daily routine.

When I moved on from dance, what I didn't anticipate was how my workout clothing options would greatly decrease. While traditional ballet dancers are often restricted to pink tights and leotards, there are a range of options for other dance disciplines like jazz, and countless color and patterned leotards for gymnasts.

As I moved into the more traditional fitness world, I was struck by the limited options available to purchase. There was a marked difference between shopping in dance stores which focused almost exclusively on women and athletic apparel and footwear stores in the mall which had much fewer options for women. Most of the clothes in the athletic stores were for men. The women's section was noticeably smaller and would typically be in the back of the store.

The women's options focused on lighter pastel colors like pink, lavender, light blue, and white. By comparison, the men's options offered blues, greens, grays, and my favorite color, black, among others. Not wanting to wear the women's options I would often try on the men's clothes, purchasing a few items but finding the sizing was off most of the time. I would also "borrow" lacrosse or basketball shorts from my father to work out in because they were loose and could be rolled up to a length I felt comfortable wearing.

For years I wore a gym uniform of a loose cotton t-shirt, lacrosse shorts, and men's sneakers to the gym. I continued to shop for women's activewear whenever possible, but never really bought much beyond a sports bra. I found many of the women's options to be too short, tight, and offered in colors I did not enjoy wearing.

Things began to change around 2005 when I started seeing basic short sleeve Under Armour performance shirts offered in women's sizes! I remember being so thrilled that the shirts fit that I immediately purchased several to replace my cotton shirts for workouts and wore one every time I went to the gym.

Around 2011, I was living in New York City and had observed that first yoga and then spin classes were increasing in popularity. As these fitness boutiques grew throughout the city, so did the presence of new activewear brands like Lululemon and Athleta. With more fit, color, and design options available, I was *finally* able to walk into a store that focused *exclusively* on women's activewear again.

Once I bought my first pair of yoga pants I realized there was no going back to wearing lacrosse shorts. The pants fit me well and made me feel good about what I was wearing. I'd wear them to the gym, the grocery store, and around my neighborhood. And, I wasn't the only one. I saw many women in the city wearing their activewear in the same places.

In 2012, I moved to North Carolina to go back to school. I also saw classmates of mine, both male and female, wearing their activewear to class as if they were everyday clothes. Being able to dress casually almost daily, I found myself shopping for activewear that I intended to wear exclusively outside the gym because it was comfortable and fit my athletic frame better than other casual clothes.

The more I wore activewear as casual clothes the more I played around with how I could mix and match casual and athletic clothes in the same outfit. Before I knew it, I had a healthy collection of activewear and sports inspired apparel from which to choose. I'd always been sporty and now I had stylish clothes that I could wear to reflect that.

Now working in a casual work environment, leggings have become part of my office wardrobe. Most days I will mix an element of activewear with street or other business casual clothes to "dress things up" for a professional environment. The more I experimented with my outfits, the more I found it possible to create comfortable and stylish work appropriate outfits.

For me, athleisure had extended beyond workout clothes, it had become a mindset about dressing in a way that allowed me to show my personal style but still be appropriate. Co-workers would comment how I looked so pulled together even though I was wearing some form of athleisure or athletic inspired clothing.

As a public debate around whether yoga pants were appropriate for women to wear outside the gym grew louder, I began chatting with women about athleisure – why they liked it and how they felt about it. After years of working in the retail industry, wearing activewear, talking with women about their clothing preferences, and paying attention to what women are wearing, I've got a few theories on how athleisure became so popular, how it has impacted women and the apparel industry, as well as how clothes will change in the future as athleisure evolves.

I've written this book to open the conversation up. There are a lot of opinions and viewpoints on athleisure, so I wanted to capture a few of them in addition to my own to understand the bigger picture around women's clothing decisions.

Instead of focusing on celebrities and high fashion, I chose to focus more on the perspectives of every day women, entrepreneurs, and brands that are driving change through the communities they are building and their influence on each other.

Each chapter of this book will debunk what I believe to be a falsehood connected with athleisure or women's apparel. While reading all of the chapters, *or falsehoods*, will provide a more complete view of influences and outcomes of athleisure, each chapter can also be read on its own, à la carte style if you will.

- The history behind athleisure and how it grew
- How and why women wear athleisure today
- The challenges associated with athleisure
- How athleisure has impacted fashion and is expected to continue evolving

My goal is for women to recognize that when they choose to wear what they want rather than what they think they should wear, they are helping to redefine what is appropriate for women to wear rather than allowing arbitrary rules or what's currently available to dictate their choices.

This book is not meant to be an exhaustive study on athletic clothing and athleisure but a collection of insights and stories to provoke thought and discussion around how women decide to dress on a daily basis.

And frankly, who doesn't want to wear comfortable clothing that easily transitions from work to the gym and makes them feel great? Based on the way clothes are trending, it appears we just may have it all where clothing is concerned.

The future of women's apparel will be run by women, for women. And, based on what I've seen so far, women's clothing is going to be a lot more functional and comfortable than clothing of the past *without* compromising style.

Women are no longer accepting subpar options, they are designing better ones. Get on board or get out of the way.

ATHLEISURE IS JUST A TREND

———

Regardless of what you call it, the athleisure trend was driven by women's decision to wear yoga pants and other activewear outside the studio. This was not the first time women had made a conscious decision to change the way they dress. I'm not talking about cosmetic changes like the preference for polka dots over stripes; I'm referring to changes that caused a cultural shift that happened as women decided to represent themselves with clothes that pushed boundaries.

Fashion isn't always just about being fabulous, it can also be used as a form of expression representing a movement or revolution. Whether a group is wearing a specific garment, outfit, or even a simple ribbon, clothing and fashion allows the wearers to communicate a message, sometimes subtly and sometimes boldly, to those outside the movement.

Athleisure isn't a *just* a trend, it represents a permanent shift in how women are deciding to dress – for themselves, their lifestyles, and comfort. And I'm not the only one who feels this way.

Observers of fashion have noted that athleisure is a form of revolt against a culture obsessed with policing women's appearance. "There's a reason that women dressing casually threatens the status quo — it's subversive and the ultimate sign of not caring. It's the quintessential 'I'm going to dress for myself' statement," fashion news editor Véronique Hyland wrote for *New York Magazine's, The CUT* in 2014.[4]

If we look at examples in history, conscious changes in the way women dress are never simply about the clothes, there is a connection between what women choose to wear and how they want to live and represent themselves. As women's lives continue to evolve, there's a need to update their clothes accordingly. The modern woman's life has become more demanding as she juggles work, family, fitness, and personal goals, and athleisure has emerged as the solution to help her navigate these demands.

---

4   (Hyland 2014)

Long before athleisure, women adjusted the way they dress to be in sync with how their lives changed or they would like them to change. There have been milestones that advanced women's clothing as well as their lifestyles and positions within society. What initially was seen as avant-garde or risqué eventually became the norm.

As women continue the fight for equality, they are also communicating the desire to dress how they want without judgement. While not the first time women have taken control over the way they dress, I believe athleisure marks the latest milestone in the women's movement fashion timeline.

Before examining athleisure throughout the rest of the book, I am going to use this chapter to discuss how women's fashion has been dictated in the past, how women have succeeded in changing it throughout the years, and how clothing changes often occur simultaneously with advancements in women's lives.

**

Historically, women's clothing was designed to be fashionable and culturally acceptable, not functional. From corsets to form fitting dresses and high heels, women's fashion focused on creating looks that aligned with the current standard of beauty.

In the 1850's, women attempted to break from restrictive clothing that consisted of tightly laced corsets, petticoat layers that could weigh over 10 pounds, and floor-length dresses that dragged in the streets and made it a challenge to move around without assistance.

Amelia Bloomer led the charge with her self-published temperance newspaper, *The Lily*. In it, Amelia encouraged women to forego corsets and wear loose bodices with baggy ankle-length pants for petticoats with knee length gowns to free themselves from restrictive clothing that would provide more movement. Associated with Amelia, the pants were nicknamed "bloomers."

Concerns that women wearing pants would lead to usurping male authority[5] put those efforts on hold until the 1890s when women were permitted to wear pants that looked like a bifurcated skirt (similar to culottes) for physical exercise. It wasn't until well into the 1970s that women were able to wear pants throughout their lives with little resistance.

In a 1977 *NY Times* article, "Feminism's Effect on Fashion," Dr. Mildred Newman, a well-known psychoanalyst said, "Until 15 years ago, I lived the life of a liberated woman in

---

5   (Cunningham 2003)

every respect except dress. It would never have occurred to me to wear pants to the office."[6]

The article's author, Carrie Donovan added, "Almost any woman over the age of 35 has the same sort of memories. Before the early '60s, we used to dress to conform to the dictates of fashion and to look "proper" for the occasion. If we did wear something out of the ordinary, it was considered very daring."

The evolution of pants continued, as they became part of women's suits. Enter the revolutionary designer, Coco Chanel.

While you may know her for the little black dress, perfume, or designer handbags, Coco Chanel led the way for women's suiting. A pioneer in her own right, Coco Chanel was one of the first visible women to wear pants publicly. In terms of design, she focused on creating designs for the modern independent woman of the 1920s who worked and enjoyed sports activities. At the time, post-war women were working to build careers within a male-dominated workplace.

Chanel's iconic two-piece suit kick started the replication of masculine design in women's apparel. Mixing elements of the male suit with feminine details, Chanel designed an

---

6   (Donovan 1977)

elegant, sophisticated, and comfortable suit for women. First offered in 1923, the Chanel suit would continue to be iterated for decades.

Fashion designer Yves Saint Laurent took women's suits a step further. Credited with starting the pantsuit trend in 1966 his 'Le Smoking' suit jacket was also styled after menswear.[7] In line with the acceptance of pants, the pantsuit was not well received at first and took some time to gain full acceptance in the workplace.

By the 1980s the power suit had gained popularity for women advancing in the workplace to look professional and be taken seriously. On the other hand, adapted from men's suits, women who wore the power suit were also criticized for trying to look like men.[8]

Despite the power suit's popularity among women in the 1980s, it wasn't until 1993 that pantsuits would be allowed on the Senate floor, a mere eight years before Hillary Clinton and her famous pantsuits would be sworn in as a U.S. Senator.

If you've done the math, that means it took nearly a hundred years for it to become acceptable for women to wear pants in

---

7   (Chang 2018)
8   (Komar 2016)

society and an additional 50 years to legally wear them as an elected official in the Senate. Let that sink in.

More than pants and suits, throughout the past hundred years female designers have helped update women's apparel to reflect the advancements in their lives. From Mary Quant's mini-skirts that symbolized sexual freedom in the 1960s to the ease women gained from wearing Diane von Fursten-berg's fashionable wrap dresses in the 1970s, women have slowly been updating their clothes to reflect who they are and how they want to live their lives.

Deirdre Clemente, a 20th century American Fashion His-torian at the University of Nevada tells her students, "that clothing trends aren't 'reflective' of change, but rather con-stitutive of change. So women didn't say 'Hey I'm sexually liberated, I need to go get a mini-skirt.' Rather in wearing the mini-skirt, they live out the identity that they are. Clothing is not reactive but *pro active*."[9]

**

Despite the updates women have already made to their wardrobes, there is room for more change. Even today, the construction and design of clothes lingers from another era.

---

9   Ibid

For example, why do many women's dresses still zip up in the back? This construction may have made sense back when most women did not live alone. However, back zippers do not bode well for the modern single professional women that must contort in creative ways to get dresses on and off or use some form of a wire hanger to assist. Moreover, reliance on another person to get dressed is simply ridiculous today.

The modern woman doesn't have time for high maintenance clothing. As of 2016, women make up nearly 57 percent of the U.S. labor force. Of these women, more than 40 percent have college degrees. Additionally, over 77 percent of mothers with kids under the age of 18 participate in the labor force, 75 percent of which are employed full time, and these numbers are only likely to increase as more women earn bachelor's degrees than men by the time they are 29 years old.[10]

Women are more than professionals, students, and mothers, they are wives, caregivers, friends, mentors, and so much more all while trying to take care of themselves as well. Women's roles have advanced, while their clothing construction has not.

---

10   (*U.S. Department of Labor Blog* 2017)

Men have largely dictated women's fashion over the past several decades, whether through design houses like Gucci, Ralph Lauren, and Christian Dior, leadership positions within apparel companies, or even the law. For example, women were fined or jailed for wearing skirts three inches above their ankles in the 1920s when hemlines were on the rise. Also, when designing women's apparel, men weren't as concerned with comfort and function as they were with how women looked. Beauty has often been prioritized over function and comfort.

Such a mindset hasn't changed enough. In 2011, Christian Louboutin, the luxury shoe designer known for his red soled high heels told *The New Yorker* about his lack of sympathy for the pain women endure while wearing high heels, stating, "The core of my work is dedicated not to pleasing women but to pleasing men."[11]

Elaborating about his distaste for comfort, Christian said, "'Comfy'— that's one of the *worst* words! I just picture a woman feeling bad, with a big bottle of alcohol, really puffy." Comfort has been positioned at odds with beauty and fashion when it comes to women's clothing, indicating a woman who has dressed comfortably has given up on her appearance and cannot be stylish.

---

11   (Collins 2011)

But, why does it have to be one or the other? Increasingly, women are striving for both comfort *and* style.

Fun fact: Heels were originally worn by men as early as the 10th century to help them remain in the stirrups while horseback riding. Associated with upper class and status, the higher the heel, the higher the social rank. Women began wearing them as well in the 1600s, while in the late 1700s men discarded them for more practical footwear options.[12]

Now women are *beginning* to ditch them as well.

Women wear heels as a symbol of femininity and style. An iconic fashion staple, high heels continue to be popularized by television shows like *Sex and the City*. However, the popularity of the high heel is fading as women are increasingly trading them for the comfort and practicality of sneakers and flats.

While I have known a handful of women that can wear heels all day without issue, most women experience pain after wearing them for a few hours. Look under any table at a wedding reception and you will find at least one pair of high heels abandoned as its owner dances the night away barefoot.

---

12   ("The Gender Bending History of The High Heel" 2014)

This shift from high heels to lower and flat alternatives was reported by the market research company NPD Group in 2017 showing high heel sales declined 11 percent while women's sneaker sales increased 37 percent.[13] Fueling the fire of this change were fashionable celebrities like Victoria Beckham, who were once known for a signature look that included stiletto heels but were increasingly seen wearing fashionable sneakers instead.

Previously a high heel addict who had stated that she "can't concentrate in flats," Victoria told *The Telegraph* in 2016, "I just can't do heels any more. At least not when I'm working. I travel a lot. Clothes have to be simple and comfortable."[14]

More public displays of celebrities trading heels for sneakers include actress Kristen Stewart ditching her Louboutin high heels after her photo op at the Cannes Film Festival in May 2018. In the past, the festival has turned away women who showed up for the screenings wearing rhinestone flats instead of the required heels. When asked about the Cannes high heel policy in 2016 Stewart told the Hollywood Reporter, "If you're not asking guys to wear heels and a dress, you can't ask me either."[15]

---

13   (Ell 2018)
14   (Chung 2016)
15   (Johnson 2018)

Out with a "Fashion is pain," motto and in with "Fashion is comfort."

**

Despite men's focus on designing looks for women that please them, women have achieved victories along the way in terms of clothes that improve their health, add ease to their lives, and reflect their increasing influence in the workforce and society.

From bloomers to high heels, women's clothing has certainly come a long way over the past couple of centuries.

Throughout history and particularly the past hundred years, women have updated their clothes to improve their health and match their evolving needs and lifestyles. With each change, women are moving closer to increased movement, freedom of self-expression, versatility, and comfort. While most of the wardrobe updates were initially met with resistance, they eventually became commonplace over time.

While the recent athleisure trend represents a marked change in the way women dress, it is not the first and won't be the last. Initially disregarded as a passing fashion trend, the fact that athleisure has not only continued to persist but grown past its anticipated expiration despite backlash indicates something more is at work.

Athleisure has grown in popularity at the same time that women's movements around gender pay, harassment, and body positivity are also center stage. Coincidence or are they related? I believe the latter.

By choosing clothes that they want to wear that meet their needs, women are communicating they are in control over their wardrobes and lives.

ATHLEISURE STARTED AS FASHION

———

The road to athleisure started long before yoga pants became a popular clothing option. It wasn't long ago that women didn't even have the option to participate in organized sports, let alone purchase clothes that supported them as athletes. Most every athletic inspired fashion trend started as a functional option first that evolved to become fashionable over time.

Believe it or not, the recent rise of athleisure isn't the first time that athletic apparel or footwear became mainstream along with fitness trends, it's just the latest. It's no coincidence that whenever women have been provided with stylish clothes or footwear that supports their exercise of choice that those options quickly become a hot commodity. When you have limited options, it's easy for something that fits your needs more closely to stand out.

Female athletes need equipment and clothing to help them perform their best, including essentials like sports bras and sneakers. Even after they were allowed on the field, female athletes haven't always been provided with suitable equipment to play. These athletes deserved more attention than they received for a long time. Before fashion, women need functional options.

Yes, athleisure has now become fashionable to wear, but the rise of its popularity is also rooted in the fact that women's athletic options were neglected for so long, and its growth is actually the women's market catching up to where it should have been all along.

**

With the popularity of exercise classes, digital fitness trackers, and the number of activewear options available to women today it's probably difficult to imagine a time when women weren't allowed to register for a marathon or a gym membership. However, it wasn't so long ago that this was true.

A *key* milestone for women in sports was when Title IX was passed in 1972 to correct gender sports program imbalances. Title IX is a federal law that prohibits discrimination based on gender in any federally funded education program or activity. Before this law, women's sports programs didn't really exist at schools and universities. However, while girl's programs didn't sprout overnight, through persistence and struggle more high school and college sports programs were created for girls in more equal measure to boys.

The impact of Title IX cannot be over-emphasized. The opportunity for girls and young women to play sports has had a ripple effect on the way women live their lives and what they set out to achieve. Many of the young female athletes grew up to be fitness-minded adults, raising their own athletes and contributing to the increased focus on living active lifestyles.

To get a sense of how much women's participation in sports has changed since Title IX check out these stats. According to the Women's Sports Foundation, before Title IX was passed 1 in 27 girls played sports, but as of 2016 two in five girls play sports.[16] Similarly, the National Federation of State High School Associations estimates the number of girls that competed in high school sports grew from 295,000

---

16   (Olmstead 2016)

in 1972 to 3.2 million in 2011.[17] In terms of collegiate sports, the number of female NCAA athletes increased from fewer than 30,000 to over 193,000 between 1972 and 2011.[18] As for adult women, Running USA estimates that 10 percent of marathon finishers were women in 1980 versus 44 percent in 2016.[19]

Women's participation in sports has more than reached critical mass. While we should never have been an afterthought, we certainly *should not* be ignored as athletes now.

So how did we get from Title IX to athleisure? Once women began to establish themselves as athletes, they obviously needed clothing options designed for women, not men, to dominate whatever exercise they chose to participate in. The accomplishments of women in sports are even more impressive when you consider their ability to participate has been limited by the lack of equipment, including the sports bra.

In hindsight, while it may seem obvious to design equipment for female athletes, up until recently most athletic apparel was made for men and retro-fitted for women...and since the athletic apparel industry was run by men, and men don't

---

17   (Lee and Dusenbery 2012)
18   Ibid
19   (The Denver Post 2017)

require sports bras, that piece of equipment wasn't exactly on their radar to create for women.

Out of necessity, the first sports bra was invented in 1977 by Lisa Lindahl and theater costume designer Polly Smith with the help of Smith's assistant, Hinda Schreiber. Similar to what many women experience, Lisa loved to run but has a larger chest and did not enjoy the discomfort that came with running. In an effort to solve her problem, the women had the idea to sew two jockstraps together, nicknaming their creation the "jockbra."

After Lisa found the initial prototype to be helpful when she ran, the women worked to improve the materials and design as well as start their own company to sell their invention. The official name for their sports bra was the Jogbra. Even though women saw a clear need for the sports bra, it took some convincing to get sporting goods stores that were most often run by men to sell them.

As Lisa recalled in a 2017 interview with a Boston radio station, "When I got the right person, he — it was always a he — and he would say, 'A bra? Why would I put a bra in my sporting goods store?' And I would look at him and I'd say, 'You carry jockstraps, don't you?'"[20] Her response was effective.

---

20   (Given 2017)

Lisa's persistence paid off. Within the first year, her company became profitable, and profits doubled for several years afterward. Considered an important invention contributing to the rise of female athletes, the Jogbra was featured as part of and an exhibit at the Smithsonian National Museum of American History in 2015. The exhibit explored the connection between women's clothing decisions, lifestyles, and their push for independence.

Part of the caption next to the bra read, "The introduction of the sports bra did more than improve athletes' performances. It represented a revolution in ready-to-wear clothing, and for many women athletes, past, present, and future, it actually made sports possible."[21]

**

More than bras, women also needed shoes and apparel to wear when working out. Men had a lot of sporty options to wear while working out as well as sportswear options for casual situations. Women, on the other hand had a lot fewer options to choose from that weren't exactly stylish. Few, if any options were created specifically for women.

---

21   (Lindahl 2018)

Despite the lack of sports apparel and footwear options, women's participation in sports kept increasing. With gyms being largely male-dominated, women looked for a way to exercise that made them feel comfortable, leading to the popularity of aerobics in the 1980s. Aerobics routines could be done in the privacy of their own homes or in groups. The woman most associated with the aerobics craze of the 80s was unequivocally Jane Fonda.

Releasing her own aerobics video *Jane Fonda's Workout* in 1982, Jane became a fitness and fashion leader with her brightly colored high cut leotard, tights, and leg warmer outfits that would define the uniform for fitness in the '80s. Even outside of aerobics, women wore leggings and leg warmers as fashion. Though exercise was about more than the clothes, through exercise women gained confidence in addition to the health benefits.

In a 1979 *Vogue* interview, Jane said, "I found early on that exercise has a tremendous effect on my morale. And when I'm working hard, I have a tendency to let everything good go. But I always hang on to my exercise. It gives me energy, staves off depression—it makes all the difference in the world."[22]

---

22 (Ruffner 2016)

However, more than tights and leotards, women needed a shoe that would work for aerobics. Running shoes are made for front to back movement, but aerobics required side-to-side agility. Women needed an aerobics shoe.

In the early 1980s, Reebok California sales representative, Angel Martinez, noticed the popularity of women's aerobics after taking classes with his wife Frankie. Similar to what happened with Lululemon 16 years later, Angel identified the aerobics trend as an opportunity to serve this community of women.

I had the opportunity to chat with Erin Narloch, the Senior Archive Manager for Reebok, about how Angel's idea was brought to life and became iconic for fitness and fashion.

Erin told me that Angel pitched the aerobics shoe idea to Reebok's Paul Fireman in March of 1982, and the classic high top Reebok Freestyle shoe went to market later that year. If you're keeping score that means it took 11 years after Title IX was passed for a sneaker to be designed specifically for women.

Through cross-promotion efforts with influential aerobics instructors like Denise Austin, popular gyms, and aerobics classes, the Freestyle became *the* aerobics shoe. The Freestyle changed everything for Reebok, skyrocketing sales from $12 million at the beginning of the '80s to $2 billion at the end of the decade.

This shoe was groundbreaking in that it not only became an iconic representation of the aerobics era but also was the first time a women's shoe preceded the creation of a men's counterpart. After the popularity of the Freestyle, the Ex-O-Fit was drafted for men off the Freestyle's design, but with an updated name because men didn't participate in aerobics, they EXercise OR engage in FITness. *This was the first time a men's shoe was launched from a women's style.*

Throughout the '80s there were key moments where the Freestyle was worn for more than aerobics, from Cybill Shepherd wearing a pair on the red carpet at the 1985 Emmy Awards to everyday women rocking a pair with their suits on the walk to work. Call it athleisure or fashion, the Freestyle became more than an aerobics shoe, it became women's go-to shoe option when they wanted to be comfortable, stylish, and sporty.

The Freestyle shoe's popularity lasted into the '90s, becoming memorialized in east coast culture through the influence of hip hop. The shoe retailed in New York City for $49.99, but after tax was $54.11. Often referred to as the 54-11 or referenced by other shoe features, the Freestyle has been mentioned in songs by DMX, Nelly, and Tiana Taylor, among others.

As recently as 2008, the popular Flo Rida featuring T-Pain song "Low" referenced the shoes with the lyric, "Them baggy sweat pants and the Reebok's with the straps." While the shoes were created for an athletic need, they came to mean more as part of popular culture and dress because of its versatile design.

**

As the popularity of aerobics cooled in the '90s, so did female focused activewear and footwear options. Even though women's participation in sports continued to rise, most of the design and product focus continued to be on men's. Women's options were largely an afterthought.

As I've already mentioned, this was around the same time that I was growing as an athlete myself, often becoming frustrated with the seemingly limited apparel and footwear options women were offered. For instance, looking at an average wall of shoes in a store, women's was most often on the side of the wall that connected with the back of the store, while men's shoe options started at the front and covered a majority of the wall.

I found the same to be true of apparel. If offered, women's options were most often found in the back of the store with a much smaller assortment then men's. Also, among the options for women I rarely found the apparel or shoes to be stylish or to fit well. The waistband for shorts would be too tight, the length would be too short...let's just say there was a lot of opportunity for women's options to be improved.

The year 1998 was a popular year for new female focused brands. Chip Wilson launched Lululemon in Canada, Scott Kerslake launched Athleta in the United States, and Tamara Hill-Norton launched Sweaty Betty in London, each of which still impact women's activewear and by extension, what's referred to as athleisure today.

LULULEMON

Chip Wilson, the founder of Lululemon, recognized the opportunity and seized it. Chip spent his early career building his surf, skate, and snowboard apparel company, Westbeach Snowboard Ltd., so he knew how to use technical fabrics for sports clothing. Selling Westbeach in 1997, Chip began looking for something else to work on. He found inspiration through yoga.

In an interview with Guy Raz for NPR's *How I Built This* podcast in 2018, Chip talked about how he came up with the idea for Lululemon and built the brand. Chip recalled how it all began saying, "I have always believed in this three times thing. So when I see something three times, then I move, and I move really quickly. So I'd seen an article in the paper about yoga. I'd seen a poster on a telephone post with a little rip-off about the yoga class. And then, I overheard a conversation in a coffee shop about yoga. And I went, wow. So, I went to this yoga class. You know, it went from about 6 to 30 people in 30 days. I was the only guy in the class."[23]

Chip recognized the next wave of a women's fitness trend and, like Angel had done over 15 years earlier, acted on it. More women were practicing yoga and there was an opportunity to create apparel for these women to wear. Beyond the yoga trend, Chip also recognized that women's lives were changing. In addition to focusing more on their fitness, women were increasingly more educated and having children later in life, leading to more disposable income.

Chip's observations about women and his technical understanding of apparel led him to found Lululemon Athletica, Inc. in 1998.

To understand what women liked and wanted to wear, Chip conducted his own research, talking with women who practiced yoga, and relied heavily on his yoga instructor, Fiona Stang, for insight and feedback about the apparel. While

---

23   (Raz 2018)

Chip set out to make technical apparel for yoga, he also recognized that women wanted style and to look good.

The recognition that women wanted their athletic clothes to perform, be stylish, and make them look good may seem obvious today, but at the time was not the common approach to women's activewear.

Moreover, Lululemon didn't advertise. Instead, the company grew organically through the fitness community and word of mouth by selling its clothing in yoga studios and focusing on design improvements. Even after opening its own stores the brand continues to update its products based on customer feedback and connects with local fitness instructors who become brand ambassadors to their community.

We all know where this story goes. Increasingly, and then all at once, women began purchasing Lululemon pants for sports other than yoga, wearing them everywhere because the clothes were also stylish. The clothes became a symbol of a fit lifestyle, regardless of whether a woman actually practiced yoga.

"Chip created functional, technical clothes that performed in yoga or anything sweaty and looked good. One such example of that combines technology with proper fabrics, Lululemon has clothing that minimizes odors produced by sweat. You went to coffee or shopping after class and did not need to change. He created this market," said Deanne Schweitzer, Lululemon's VP of Design in 2012.[24]

After years of being an afterthought, women had a brand that focused on what they liked, wanted, and needed while exercising. In response, women supported the brand with purchases and spread the word to other women about their new favorite yoga pants. Lululemon went public in 2007, doubling sales between 2010 and 2016 and growing sales 12.5 percent from 2016 to 2017.[25] Sales for the 2017 fiscal year were over $2.6 billion.

Love Lululemon or not, one cannot deny that many women love the way the product looks, feels, and performs because they have unknowingly had a hand in creating it through their feedback. Which, to that point, I've spoken with women who initially avoided the brand for various reasons but have since become customers after testing the apparel and finding it fit and performed better than alternatives.

---

24 (Mink 2012)
25 (Roberts 2017)

ATHLETA

Athleta was also launched in 1998 after its founder, Scott Kerslake, a surfer and cyclist, listened to his friends complain about a lack of fashionable athletic apparel for women during long bicycle rides. The women wanted the apparel to perform but also be able to be worn elsewhere.

"Historically, what had been available to women were items based on a men's item that were just made smaller and turned a flattering color like pink," said Scott Key, SVP and General Manager of Athleta in 2011. "Women athletes expected more."[26]

Initially, Athleta catalogs featured curated products from other brands like Patagonia and adidas. Seeing an opportunity to create better product, Scott created his own label for running, hiking, tennis, cycling, golf, yoga, and swimming. Women appreciated the focus on color, patterns, and detail. It wasn't long before the store took off, bringing in $18 million in 2001 and $30 million two years later.[27]

Purchased by Gap, Inc. in 2008, Athleta, which has become a key player in women's activewear along with Gap's other

---

26   (Pasquarelli 2011)
27   (Warner 2003)

brands – GapFit and Old Navy Active – was projected in 2017 to hit $1 billion in revenue over the next few years.[28]

Going beyond apparel, Athleta has evolved into a purpose-driven brand led by its mission to ignite a community of active, healthy, confident women and girls. Throughout this book you'll read how the brand has lived this mission through its Power of She campaign for women, the launch of Athleta Girl to inspire the next generation, and its sustainability efforts through acquiring B Corp certification.

SWEATY BETTY

Sweaty Betty launched in 1998 as well in London by Tamara Hill-Norton. Like Scott and Chip, Tamara also saw a gap in the market for stylish activewear for women who led active lifestyles. Her goal was to create activewear that would empower women and make them feel amazing through an active lifestyle.

When Sweaty Betty first opened, it sold other brands. The store rolled out its own private label line in 2009, and that's when things really took off and the business became profitable. Comfortable, functional, stylish, and flattering clothes

---

28   (Sherman 2018)

that could be worn throughout the day resonated with women.

In 2013, Sweaty Betty opened its first two U.S. stores in New York.[29] As of 2018, Sweaty Betty operates and is sold in over 60 stores across England and the United States, in addition to 25 Nordstrom locations.

The name Sweaty Betty came from a play on words. In the late '90s the fitness craze was beginning to take off in Britain but "it was not cool to sweat," said Tamara. Using that insight, she injected some fun into the brand while paying tribute to exercise-obsessed Americans with a nod to the "cool girl" from the Archie comics, Betty.[30]

Talking about the goal of the brand with Nordstrom in 2018, Tamara said, "We want women to feel powerful and motivated to live an active lifestyle. With this in mind, we have an in-house female design team that creates all of our pieces to fit, flatter, and look amazing from studio to street. We also test each piece multiple times in our London office to ensure they really perform. We actually have a saying with fabric: if we can't find it, we make it."[31]

---

29 (Kansara 2014)
30 (Price 2016)
31 (Karlstrom 2018)

Reflecting on how far their mission has come since Sweaty Betty opened its first store, Tamara also told Nordstrom, "The industry has completely changed since I started Sweaty Betty. Working out has become much cooler. Women's activewear has gone from a small area at the back of a men's gym to all of these amazing boutique studios."

**

Title IX helped accelerate women's participation in sports. For decades, women had fought for the right to participate in sports and be taken seriously as athletes. In many cases, women are still working to be seen as equal, including the equipment they use.

From the Jogbra in the 1970s, to the Reebok Freestyle in the 1980s, to stylish Lululemon yoga pants in the late 1990s, women's need for functional clothes to wear to participate in their chosen fitness activity or sport drove advancements for women's athletic clothing.

However, beyond function, the popularity of the Freestyle and Lululemon happened because the design of the options lent the products to be worn outside the gym as part of a woman's active lifestyle or as fashion. Function drove creation; the design drove its popularity.

Athleisure happened because women liked the design of the athletic options so much they found other ways to wear them, including as fashion. Good design is universal.

ATHLEISURE IS EASY TO DEFINE

———

The word athleisure is a blend of the two words, *athletic* and *leisure.*

Officially added to the Merriam-Webster dictionary in 2016, athleisure is defined as *"casual clothing designed to be worn both for exercising and for general use."*

I'll admit it, wearing athletic clothes for exercise or casually is not a new concept. Throughout the past, several clothing items originally created for sport have become casual options worn for general use. For instance, where do you think the polo shirt came from? Polo, perhaps?

Athletes have been wearing their sports clothes casually for years, as have sport fans and anyone with a sporty or street-style. Hence, there's an entire category of clothing called *sportswear*, which are clothes also designed for activity but worn casually.

The *slight nuance* with athleisure is that style met technical clothing in a way that hadn't been done before at scale. Typically, athletic clothing was focused on athletic performance while sportswear evolved to be focused on fashion and street style. Athleisure was stylish clothing for athletes that was then also worn casually like fashion.

As the popularity of athleisure grew and more designers, retailers, and new brands launched their own version of athleisure, the focus shifted from athletes to fashion. Yoga pants are being paired with sportswear bomber jackets and streetwear oversized t-shirts. Workout clothes are being worn to work that have never been sweat in. Luxury fashion brands are launching their own sneakers.

This change has ruffled the feathers of some in the athletic industry who believe the emphasis on fashion over function diminishes the true nature of activewear to improve athletic performance.

Whatever you want to call it, sport inspired lifestyle clothing is seemingly *everywhere* now. Eventually, there won't be a need to define or discuss the definition of athleisure because athletic inspired clothing will simply be just another clothing option to choose from.

**

Let's take a brief tour of the past to show why the concept of wearing athletic clothing casually isn't necessarily new. I'll start with the creation of sportswear, *the original athleisure,* and work to the start of athleisure. Please note the following is a *very* high-level overview of sportswear that is meant to be illustrative, *not* exhaustive.

Throughout the history of sports and fashion, there are several clothing styles and footwear that transitioned from sports to fashion. We've already seen how this happened with the Reebok Freestyle. The sneaker was created for aerobics but became iconized as a part of fashion and hip hop culture.

Going over a hundred years back, women were a driving force behind some of the first sportswear styles, like bloomers, starting in the 1900s. First created for sport use only and adapted from men's styles, women's sportswear evolved to be more leisure and fashion focused. Sportswear took two paths, one towards fashion and casual attire; the other focused on sports and function.

The essence of fashion is the use of inspiration to create something new, and that is exactly what designers did. Fashion sportswear was designed as an easy and functional option for modern women to wear as sport spectators, travel, and eventually every day. Early designers took elements of athletic clothing, like movement and function, and created dresses, skirts, suits and other clothes that offered a more relaxed fit and feel.

For instance, we've already mentioned how Coco Chanel used jersey fabric to create suits for women and advanced pants as more acceptable for women to wear. Leading an active lifestyle, Coco was known for designing sporty clothing options for women. Her use of jersey knit fabric was different because of its stretch, making her clothes more comfortable to wear. If you think about how a t-shirt stretches compared to a traditional woven button down shirt you'll get the idea.

Fast-forward a few decades, between 1970 and the 2000s, fashion designers, including Calvin Klein, Ralph Lauren, Donna Karan, and Norma Kamali offered relaxed and fashionable sportswear options like button downs, jersey dresses, and suits, among others. Other times sportswear took more directly from sport, adapting polo shirts and sweatshirts to be more stylish.

The other more obvious and athletic sportswear path focused on developing technical fabrics and designs for athletes. From the Champion Reverse Weave sweatshirt created in the 1940s, to the Nike Waffle Shoe that debuted in 1974, to Under Armour's HeatGear® T-shirt first offered in 1996, to Lululemon yoga pants launched in 1998, these clothes were designed for all aspects of sport and fitness. Function was the priority, not fashion.

Not limited to clothes used during exercise, sportswear also includes what athletes wear while traveling and warming up, like sweatshirts and tracksuits. Beyond athletes, sports fans wear sportswear like sweatshirts, shirts, and jackets in support of their favorite team whether at the game, a team bar, or at home watching. And, let's be honest, these same clothes are also worn by anyone who simply wants to wear comfortable clothes at home.

Driven by sport and fashion for decades, the 1970s ushered in new influences on all sportswear and an even greater shift towards athletic clothes being worn for casual use.

Streetwear originated in the late 1970s through the Los Angeles surf culture by Shawn Stussy, a surfboard designer who began selling printed t-shirts with his trademark signature, Stüssy. Rooted in skate and surf culture, streetwear's vibe had a punk, new wave, and heavy metal edge. The shirts, pants, and sweatshirts were baggier and longer than options offered by sports brands or fashion designers. Stüssy and other skate and surf brands became popular in the '90s with the rise in grunge music.

On the other coast, by the late '80s and into the '90s, hip hop culture in New York City also began influencing fashion sportswear brands like Tommy Hilfiger and Nautica. New brands were also launched, including FUBU, Rocawear, Sean Jean, Phat Farm, and Baby Phat that captured the hip hop style from sports related clothing like polo shirts and track suits to casual and more formal clothing like jeans, sweaters, and suits. These clothes weren't worn for sport, they were worn for style.

Athletic sportswear and hip hop culture also merged. For example, in 1986 the hip hop group Run DMC released the record, "my adidas" that spoke about their passion for the brand's sneakers. This led to a partnership between Run DMC and adidas, mixing art and sports in a way that ushered in athletic street fashion and created the first non-athletic collaboration with a sports brand.[32]

---

32 ("History" 2018)

As you can see, art, fashion, sports, culture, and design all influenced the evolution of athletic clothes and sportswear. Long before stylish yoga pants, and what's now referred to as athleisure, there were other athletic clothes that also became casual clothing, like the tracksuit. Born in the '60s for athletes to wear before and after exercise, Bruce Lee helped tracksuits became fashionable to wear in the '70s after wearing them on his television show and in his movies. Additionally, the popularity of disco led to the popularity of the velour track suit.

In the '80s, the tracksuit evolved into a shellsuit made of thinner and breathable fabric that was worn by athletes for exercise. At the same time, hip hop culture adopted all forms of tracksuits, from breakdancers to being featured in movies and worn by artists like The Beastie Boys and LL Cool J.

In the '90s, artists like Jay Z and Sporty Spice continued the evolution of tracksuit style sporting various athletic brands and styles while sports teams continued to be seen in shell-suits for major sports events like the Olympics. In the 2000s, Jennifer Lopez helped velour tracksuits make a comeback beyond the hip hop community when she chose to *keep it real* and sport a Juicy Couture suit in her 2001 "I'm Real" music video with Ja Rule. Her decision led to women across the country sporting one of their own as casual style.

So yes, wearing sports clothing in a casual or fashionable way isn't new. Athleisure is simply the latest chapter of athletic clothing history. And like the past, what began as technical athletic apparel expanded into fashion in a way that blurred the line between athletic and casual clothing.

The reach of athleisure expanded far beyond a group, the fashion industry, or top athletic apparel brands. Like movements before it, athleisure inspired the launch of new athletic brands and styles across the fashion and retail industry.

**

Newer brands like Lululemon, Athleta, and Sweaty Betty, in addition to growing fitness trends (I dig into this in a later chapter) grew in popularity throughout the 2000s. However, it wasn't until the early 2010s that the popularity of athletic clothing exploded, and the name athleisure was created to describe what was initially thought to be a passing trend.

Here are some stats to help paint the picture. A report by Morgan Stanley showed that sports apparel and footwear sales jumped 42 percent to $270 billion in the seven years prior to 2015.[33] In 2015, total apparel sales increased 2 percent year over year while activewear sales surged with a 16

---

33   ("Athletic Lifestyles Keep Apparel Sales Healthy" 2015)

percent increase. Without the increase in activewear, total apparel sales would have been down 2 percent, showing the shift towards active apparel from more traditional apparel categories like dress shirts, formal trousers, and tailored clothes.[34]

In 2018, reports released by the NPD group show that the athleisure segment now makes up 24 percent of total U.S. apparel sales and is only expected to grow. As the popularity of athleisure became undeniable, more brands entered the athletic clothing market while popular retailers launched their own activewear lines.

Before everyone knew it, athleisure was *everywhere.* Current brands continue to grow while retailers that had not offered athletic clothing before are releasing their own athleisure collections and new brands are being launched that offer technical and stylish options.

"There's been a notable change in women's retail, with every single brand—from H&M to Zara—having sportswear within their mix," Alison Stewart, VP of global brand strategy at adidas told *Fast Company* in 2016, "There are more and more players coming in."[35]

---

34   (Trefits Team 2016)
35   (Segran 2016a)

Focusing on options for women, new activewear brands that have launched and grown a following include Outdoor Voices, Alo, Fabletics, LNDR, MICHI, Koral, and P.E Nation, among others. These brands offer everything from leggings and tops to sweatshirts, jackets, and accessories like gym bags.

Retailers have also launched their own activewear private brands like JoyLab by Target, CALIA by Carrie Underwood at DICK'S Sporting Goods, and Zella by Nordstrom, or added activewear to their store offering, including GapFit by Gap and Old Navy Active.

And of course, central to the growth are top athletic apparel brands like Nike, adidas, Under Armour, Puma, and Reebok that continue to launch new designs and include more style into their designs over time. Similarly, outdoor brands like The North Face, Patagonia, and Columbia Sportswear continue innovating better tech fabrics for their apparel while growing in popularity as a casual clothing option as well.

One of the main ways style and fresh designs have been released is through collaborations between pairings of brands, artists, designers, athletes, and celebrities. A few sports brand collaborations have included adidas and Stella McCartney, Misty Copeland and Under Armour, and Fenty Puma by

Rihanna. Retailer collaborations have included J. Crew and New Balance and designer Alexander Wang and H&M.

The first time a fashion designer teamed with a leading global sportswear company was when designer Yohji Yamamoto and adidas collaborated on the first Y-3 line. In 2000, Yohji Yamamoto felt that "Fashion had become so boring," as he told *i-D* in 2016. "At the time, New York businessmen were starting to walk to work in their suits and sneakers. I found this strange mix incredibly charming, a fascinating hybrid that completely inspired me."[36]

Yohji reached out to adidas to ask if he could borrow some sneakers for his fall/winter 2000 show and the connection turned into a collaboration. In 2002 the first Y-3 collection launched. The result was a game-changing modern collection that was perfectly timed. "We created something that did not exist before and completely projected the future," Yohji told *i-D*.

Y-3 mixed light and soft fabrics with breathable technology for running tights, jackets, and tops that are perfect for working out but never compromised style. The collection's footwear design director summed up why the collaboration has been so successful for the past 15 years, stating "It's a tension between Yohji and adidas. If it's too adidas, it doesn't work. If

---

36   (Shackleton 2016)

it's too Yohji, you can buy that already from Yohji. It's when these two things that shouldn't go together, do come together, you create something new."[37]

The success of this collaboration led to others, including adidas and Stella McCartney a year later. This and other collaborations showed that fashion, sport, and culture could come together in a way that appealed to a larger audience.

Holly Downes, who founded her own women's activewear brand Ethona and worked as an activewear designer for over ten years told me how she noticed the shift in fashion towards activewear over the past few years.

She said, "Now you can look at WGSN [a fashion industry trend service] and can see influence coming from activewear where ten years ago it was coming from couture. To see Chanel on the runway with tennis shoes and iridescent piercing is just so cool to see that it has totally flipped." Or rather, is it simply a return to Coco Chanel's sporty style, but updated for the modern woman? Fashion *is* cyclical.

Beyond Chanel, several other luxury brands have also released their own fashionable athleisure lines including Balenciaga, Celine, Gucci, and Louis Vuitton to name a few.

---

37 (Spagnolo 2018)

The volume of athletic clothing options available and how they were being worn as casual clothing helped fuel the popularity of what was named athleisure. Athleisure became a go-to casual clothing option worn on weekends, to run errands, attend low-key events, and even wear in casual work environments.

In reference to its definition, whether athleisure clothes have or will ever be worn for exercise has become less of a focus. Instead of focusing on athletes, athleisure has become increasingly focused on fashion, similar to sportswear. A 2014 market research study revealed that nearly half of the people surveyed admit purchasing activewear for "nonactive use, as casual and everyday wear."[38]

As fashion designer Alexander Wang, known for his urban style and collaborations said in reference to this shift, "I live in gym clothes. When you go out on the street, it's the uniform now."[39]

Completing that uniform was footwear, which was also impacted by athleisure. In a 2018 report about U.S. athletic footwear, Matt Powell, VP and Senior Industry Advisor for The NPD Group, Inc. spoke to the popularity of casual

---

38   (Studeman 2014)
39   Ibid

athletic sneaker options saying, "I often get asked whether the bubble around leisure will burst anytime soon, and the answer is no. There is not a single performance shoe in the top ten list for 2017, which illustrates the sportswear fashion cycle we are in. Athleisure rules the runway, and the line between what is an athletic shoe and a casual shoe continues to blur. Brands and retailers must continue to feed this trend."[40]

Similar to what happened with apparel, top athletic brands responded to the surge in sneaker popularity, as did fashion and other shoe brands. The resurrection of '90s trends led to a surge in popularity of classic and original sneaker styles like the adidas Superstar, Nike Cortez, Puma Suedes, Vans Classic Slip-On, Converse All Stars, and of course the Reebok Freestyle, among many other brands and styles. Beyond original styles, new styles continued to be released including the Nike Air VaporMax and adidas NMD, that helped the popularity of sneakers even further.

Expanding sneaker options further, fashion labels like Balenciaga led the popularity of the "dad sneaker" trend (sneakers with a chunky sole) with their Triple S shoe, while designers like Kanye West couldn't keep his fashionable Yeezy sneakers in stock.

---

40 (The NPD Group, Inc. 2018)

**

So, with the incredible athletic apparel and footwear sales growth coupled with the increasing focus on the fashionability over the functionality of athletic clothing, what does the athletic apparel industry think about athleisure? Based on what I found, the word athleisure is virtually ignored and not well received.

In fact, the word athleisure is not used by athletic brands while it is used by fashion focused retailers that sell those same brands. For instance, while retailers like Nordstrom and TJ Maxx have made reference to athleisure on their ecommerce sites, you will not see athleisure mentioned on any of the top athletic brand websites or sporting goods retailers like Dick's Sporting Goods.

There's a reason for the dislike. The athletic apparel and footwear industry doesn't like the word athleisure because it's perceived to dilute the focus on technical apparel created to support and improve an athlete's performance to a fashion trend. Athletic apparel is seen as wearable technology that athletes wear to perform their best, which can be attractive but isn't the driving focus of the clothes.

However, even though they don't reference athleisure, athletic brands do acknowledge that their clothes are worn for casual use as well and that style is an important component to the design.

In a *Business of Fashion* 2015 article discussing women's sportswear fashion, then Nike president Trevor Edwards is quoted as saying, "We are seeing growth in the performance segments — running and training — and in terms of the style and look that comes from that. Tights are the new denim. We have seen that women interact more seamlessly across running, workout, fitness, and lifestyle. We see all those things blend." He went on to say, "One of the things that we recognize, certainly in the women's business, is that there is no performance without style."[41]

Alternatively, others in the industry have been more direct about their distaste for the word athleisure and its impact. In a *Women's Wear Daily* article regarding the erosion of performance focus, Christine Day, who first worked as an executive at Lululemon and now works with adidas, summed up this viewpoint well.

"I really absolutely hate that word. In some ways, it's kind of demeaning. It means that women aren't really serious athletes, they're just wearing clothes that look like they're athletic. When you live in just ath-leisure, there's permission to

---

41   (Mellery-Pratt 2015)

take quality down…it's permission to commoditize it. That's what I find kind of offensive, meaning you're not serious about working out, but also taking quality down to a level where it isn't really performance."[42]

Similarly, the "godfather of athleisure" and founder of Lululemon himself, Chip Wilson, weighed in as well in an April 2018 *Forbes* article. Titled, "Why the Word 'Athleisure' is Misunderstood," Chip noted that the term athleisure is "a term made popular by the New York-based fashion industry 20 years after Lululemon got its start. It describes a category of clothing meant to look athletic, but with no inherent technical function. Put simply, it's the antithesis of the business I love."[43]

Explaining further he writes, "Lululemon's success came out of creating high-performance technical clothing that stood up to the test of elite athletes — and was beautiful enough to wear for everyday life. The 'athletic-look' fashions that have popped up in its wake have muddied the waters of real technical apparel and left consumers, analysts, and investors confused. It's time to set the record straight."

On the other side of the fence are the brands that focus more equally on the functionality and fashionability of their

---

42   (Clark 2016)
43   (Wilson 2018)

activewear. These creators are calling for a new term or category that incorporates the aesthetic element not included in the original athleisure definition.

Jennifer Bandier, founder of the fashion activewear retailer Bandier, which sells many of the new stylish activewear brands as well as some of the top athletic brands, discussed her desire for the term to disappear in an interview with *Fast Company* in 2018. Jennifer said, "by partnering with designers on active pieces that are equally glamorous and high performance, we have an opportunity to create a new category in fashion. We created the term 'Active Fashion' as a way to truly describe how the modern woman wants to dress."[44]

Another term may only confuse the situation even further. Instead, I believe there is a room for both technical and fashion-focused apparel just as there was room for athletic and fashionable sportswear. Athletes will continue to need technical options while casual-focused wearers will be looking for fashionable options. As history has shown there isn't one way to design athletic clothing.

**

_____

44 (Segran 2016b)

So, what is athleisure and how do you define it? Apparently, it depends on whom you ask and what their point of reference is. For such a seemingly simple definition, athleisure sure does cause confusion and frustration.

As we'll discuss throughout the rest of this book, changes in lifestyle, preferences, and mindset around how clothes should feel, fit, and look have shifted clothing decisions toward athletic and athletic inspired options, regardless of how they are classified.

Clothes designed for working out now require an element of style as well as performance because they are being worn for leisure only more often. At the same time, as we'll get to later, technical fabric and athletic design is also being incorporated into non-athletic clothing.

Regardless of what it's called, most everyone recognizes that the lines between athletic clothes and fashion have blurred. Athleisure marks the latest timestamp of athletic clothes evolving into comfortable every day clothes.

ATHLEISURE IS BRAND DRIVEN

Athleisure was a way of dressing that grew organically through communities. There wasn't a marketing campaign that urged women to "wear yoga pants to brunch," some women just started doing it. And when women saw those women wearing yoga pants outside the gym, they started wearing them on the street as well.

This dramatic explanation is a classic fashion adoption case where early innovators push the boundaries of a trend until more adopt it and the trend becomes ubiquitous. In athleisure's case, the popularity of the style grew largely through word of mouth among women, increasingly becoming more conversational with brands as they responded to what women were wearing.

Through communities, women exchange information and opinions as well as provide support. Women trust the opinions of each other to help make purchase decisions. Opinions and feedback are not only shared with each woman's friends and family in the moment but are also shared with all of her followers and her friends' followers on social media.

This added element of social media and transparent feedback has created an interesting dynamic between women, fitness studios, activewear brands, and the digital world, where they are all influencing each other to a degree.

Call it omni-channel, an eco-system, or something else, there's now an interactive and dynamic dialogue between women, brands, and their communities. Women are influencing as much as they are being influenced.

**

Starting with communities that are built more the old-fashioned way, female athletes build relationships with their fellow comrades through sweat. Women enjoy being a part of fitness communities for motivation, support, and accountability. As evidenced by the popularity of boutique fitness classes and trends of the past, many women enjoy working out in a group. Beyond the health benefits, attending class is an opportunity for women to be social and build relationships.

So, how did athleisure even become a thing? Well, as you know, from aerobics in the '80s to STEP Reebok workouts in the '90s to yoga, Pilates, barre, and spin classes that emerged in the 2000s, fitness trends have influenced women's focus on fitness and the associated fashion many times over the past few decades.

Further contributing to the most recent fitness trends was a generational shift. Millennial women were the first generation to grow up in a post-Title IX world, the first of which were moving into adulthood around the same time that athleisure began to take off in the late 2000s, choosing to focus on different priorities than previous generations. A 2016 Harris poll found that 72 percent of millennials prefer to spend their money on experiences rather than material things.[45]

Spoiler alert, exercise counts as an experience. Instead of heading to happy hour after work, women head to a fitness class, and after the fitness class, they may head to a fast casual restaurant together to pick up some dinner. Alternatively, on

---

45   (Trefis 2016)

the weekend women run errands before or after class where other women see their athleisure outfits. After seeing enough women sporting athleisure around town, new women begin doing the same.

In addition to the social experience, the community built in the gym also keeps women coming back. The ability to build communities has been the foundation for so many of the now popular fitness studios, like Pure Barre, which is most known for its total body workouts using the ballet barre and floor.

Founded in 2001 by dancer, choreographer, and fitness guru Carrie Rezabek Dorr, what started out as a studio in the basement of an office in Birmingham, Michigan, has grown to 460 studios and communities across the U.S. and Canada.

I've seen firsthand how fitness studios have become part of women's lives and resulting clothing choices. When I attended school in Durham, North Carolina, a Pure Barre studio opened in the fall of 2013. Even before the studio opened, Pure Barre was one of the most popular topics of conversation, particularly among my female classmates.

It felt like *everyone* was excited. Women who had taken Pure Barre classes before moving to Durham shared their experience with women who had not. The resounding theme was that many of my female classmates were going to try a class as soon as the studio opened.

After opening, the conversation moved to discussing which classes everyone was able to get into or what number they were on the waitlist, how many classes they had attended that week, and how sore they all were from taking class.

To put it lightly, the studio created a fitness frenzy over night. Social plans were being made around everyone's Pure Barre schedule. Women that had never stepped foot on our campus gym were attending Pure Barre classes two and three times a week. My classmates were comparing "war stories" about how difficult the exercises were and how much they loved the challenge. "I didn't even know I had a muscle there!" was commonly heard around campus.

Many of my female classmates kept attending classes through graduation the following year. And of course, several of them also purchased apparel from the studio. And while my classmates were already wearing some form of athleisure in the classroom, once Pure Barre entered the mix, the percent of women wearing athleisure increased so much that I felt over-dressed if I didn't attend class in athleisure.

**

Another woman who knows the power of a fitness community is Laura Deitch who owns a Pure Barre studio in Mechanicsburg, Pennsylvania. The Pure Barre community has not only influenced how Laura became a Pure Barre owner, but also how she runs her business. Laura initially became aware of Pure Barre while living in NYC after a friend of hers opened a studio where a different friend also taught classes. Wanting to support both of her friends, Laura attended a class and became a regular.

After opening her studio Laura realized the importance of developing and nurturing her community to grow and sustain her business, taking note that women who attended her classes would go out to coffee together, keep each other accountable to attend class, and develop relationships outside the studio.

To build her community, Laura made it a point to invest in her clients, telling me, "It's important to me to get to know my clients and customers. I want to know their names and get to know who they are." Laura also gets involved with the local community through fitness events.

Like other Pure Barre studios, Laura dedicates a section of her studio for retail, selling fashionable activewear. She selects what styles to sell in her store based on past client feedback, and how the pieces are likely to perform both in class and as part of women's lifestyles.

Most of the brands are not easily found at other local retailers and tend to be stylish, so women aren't always familiar with them and tend to have a lot of questions about the activewear. To help her members overcome any apprehension about investing in new activewear, Laura wears new styles and brands around the studio to show clients how they perform and look on a real woman.

She has found that once women see the product on someone they are more likely to purchase it, and once purchased, women quickly realize the value of their investment and are likely to purchase more items. All of Laura's efforts to build and engage with her studio and local community have paid off. After just two years, she is already making plans to open a second studio.

In addition to Pure Barre, there are *many* other fitness studios that also have loyal communities of women, including CorePower Yoga, Soul Cycle, Flywheel, and Orange Theory to name a few. And, now that there are subscription membership options like ClassPass that allow the option to take classes across many exercise options including yoga, strength training, barre, martial arts, Pilates, boxing, and indoor cycling classes, and health clubs, women and men are able to be a part of many communities.

**

Fitness studios aren't the only exercise game around. Other fitness trends like CrossFit, Barry's Bootcamp, running, and various other sports clubs are popular among women as well as men.

The same rules around community and fitness apply for these exercise programs and sports. As Rachel Rucker, who has been part of the CrossFit community for ten years told me, "As I became more involved with CrossFit, a camaraderie formed, similar to what I had when I played sports in high school but didn't get from working out at a regular gym. I like having a community of people looking for me to show up."

From what she told me, most of Rachel's workout clothes are a mix of CrossFit related brands she receives at events or other athletic brands she buys because she likes the way they look and work for the gym. She purchases activewear to work out in, to relax in, and run errands in. Athleisure style is based on the athlete's needs and preferences. Some want more function while others want more fashion.

Moreover, today's communities are extending beyond physical communities, they've gone digital. From popular online programs like Beach Body, Daily Burn, and Shaun T's *Insanity* workout to communities built by trainers themselves such as Kayla Itsines, Massy Arias, to Tone It Up founders Katrina Scott and Karena Dawn, women and men can stream workouts and be a part of a community of fellow members online through Facebook groups, online discussion boards, and social media.

Whether it's yoga, a run club, CrossFit, or an online program, each has a community to be a part of and equipment and apparel for purchase. The ability for athletic brands to connect with the fitness communities has proven to be a successful formula. From the Freestyle's connection with aerobics in the 1980s to Lululemon's connection with yoga in the 2000s, both connected with top fitness instructors to be brand advocates early on.

Traditional marketing works, but engagement with fitness communities works better. As seen consistently with many brands, creating relationships with local and/or popular fitness instructors through sponsored classes and clothing provides visibility for the brand and helps build its community.

**

I have also experienced how fitness, fashion, and communities overlap to influence purchase decisions and involvement. Similar to Lululemon, Athleta stores also engage with their local store communities through fitness classes often hosted by local brand ambassadors. Each store posts its events online where anyone can sign up to attend.

Not one to pass up a free or inexpensive fitness class, I have attended a couple of the events. Preferring to share my experiences with other women, I talked a co-worker of mine, Allyson, into attending the event with me. The first event we attended was hosted by a local brand ambassador at the yoga studio where she teaches followed by a trunk show featuring Athleta items.

After successfully completing the yoga session, the Athleta representative raffled off a free outfit and as luck would have it my name was chosen. Being a person who never wins a raffle and buys a lot of activewear, I was *thrilled*. I gave my information to the same Athleta representative to schedule a future shopping date.

Allyson and I then shopped the trunk show selection of Athleta clothes. Before the event, Allyson had never shopped the brand. She told me that most of her workout clothes were purchased from another retailer and she never wore them outside the gym because they weren't particularly stylish.

As we were shopping through the rack of clothes I hear, "This is not athletic wear, you are a liar! This is the softest fabric I have ever felt!" Bursting out in laughter, I turned to see Allyson holding up one of the sweatshirt tops which she ended up purchasing that evening. Beyond the fabric, Allyson loved the design that included a cross-cross hem. It was a *fancy* sweatshirt.

Fast forward to the free outfit day and Allyson came with me again. As I shopped for my outfit, she shopped an Athleta store for the first time. Not surprisingly, we both left with purchases. However, to my surprise, the next day at work Allyson told me that she had gone online at home and purchased even more items that weren't available in her size at the store.

A short time later I asked Allyson if she liked her new clothes. She told me, "They hold up well for a workout and are stylish enough to wear in other situations. I don't feel disgusting after a workout, I feel like I could leave the gym and run an errand in them versus other clothes I've worn in the past. They make me feel good."

There it was, the power of community influence combined with stylish and comfortable clothing options. Athleisure had gained a new card-carrying member.

**

Beyond fitness communities and local stores, social media allows women to influence each other at scale and has been a driving force behind its growth and the rise of new brands. Between hashtags, tagging, community pages, commenting, and direct messaging, there are many ways for women to connect with each other on social media and online.

As of late 2018, female users in the U.S. make up 68 percent of the 500 million Instagram users,[46] 70 percent of the 163 million Snapchat users,[47] 44 percent of the 2.2 billion Facebook users,[48] and 34 percent[49] of the 336 million Twitter users.[50] Additionally, 81 percent of the 250 million Pinterest users are female.[51] In aggregate, women make up half of users overall but clearly have their preferred apps.

Also, beyond social media, other online communities are important as well. Sixty-nine percent of Millennial Moms

---

46   (Aslam 2018a)

47   (Iqbal 2018)

48   (Dogtiev 2018)

49   ("Twitter: Number of Monthly Active U.S. Users 2010-2018" 2018)

50   ("Global Twitter User Distribution as Of October 2018, By Gender" 2018)

51   (Aslam 2018b)

use blogs to inform purchasing decisions, while 64 percent use other social platforms.[52]

So, how influential are online communities and information on women's purchase decisions? According to a report by Merkle and Levo, while 83 percent of the women surveyed said that customer ratings and reviews influenced their purchase decisions, 60 percent are influenced by friends and family recommendations, 33 percent by word of mouth, and while 25 percent of decisions are shaped by influencers and Instagrammers, 62 percent have tried a brand based on an influencer's recommendation.[53]

Okay, enough with the stats. What does all of this mean? Well first, reaching women at scale has gotten a lot more complicated than the good old days when brands launched big television ads and ran an ad in the newspaper. Women are interacting with each other on various social media apps, checking blog sites, and sharing their own opinions.

Plus, each woman has her own mix of friends, family and other women she connects with through these networks that she is entertained by, motivated by or interested in for various other reasons. Media interaction today is driven by

52 ("Women Are Driving the Social Media Revolution". 2018)
53 ("Millennial Women Have Strong Purchasing Power. What Influences It? – Marketing Charts" 2018)

women and what they want to see and less so by what brands want to show them.

This has made it even easier for women to connect with each other. All they have to do is search a few hashtags to find a group of women with similar interests. When it comes to clothes and fitness, women are able to connect with trainers, stylists, and other everyday women to learn or share workout tips, exercises, as well as outfit and style ideas or anything one can think of.

Today, social media influencers, or women that have established an audience and credibility in a specific area, influence their community with their ideas, thoughts, and opinions. Now instead of sharing their thoughts with a few of their friends over lunch, women are sharing their opinions with a few hundred of their "friends."

In some ways influencers and bloggers are like a go-to friend that knows a lot about a particular area, so you ask them for their opinion because you trust what they have to say. Through social media, blogs, and other online communities, women are able to connect with women who share their interests, influencers, and even the brands themselves to reach out to with comments, feedback, or questions.

Caitlin Kane, a woman in her late 20s talked with me about how she engages with influencers. "All of the women I follow are models or athletes. I'm inspired by their outfits, what they wear, and how they show different ways of wearing things that you don't necessarily think of." Telling me how she finds people to follow outside of her friends and family she told me, "I usually find people to follow through clicking around, they'll be featured somewhere, and one thing leads to another."

Based on how much she likes what her favorite influencers wear, Caitlin may choose to purchase clothes she sees them wear. I find this to be true of many women I spoke with. Women follow influencers or bloggers whose style they like or want to be inspired by.

In addition, while celebrities and top influencers may have tens or hundreds of millions of followers, influencers with smaller audiences in the thousands, or *micro-influencers*, have been found to have greater impact than influencers with millions of followers, particularly among younger customers.

To put this in high school terms, women are more likely to follow the opinions of the most popular girl in school over the pop singer they have a poster of in their room.

"Younger generations like Millennials and Gen Z respond to more 'real' influencers over celebrities and gravitate to the candid and authentic nature" of those influencers who are able to embrace the rawness of a non-filtered life, Sarah Owen, WGSN's senior editor of digital media & marketing, told *Fashionista* in 2018.[54] These women are more influential because they are more relatable.

This is a lesson that has also translated into sports. Women are more likely to be influenced by women they connect with than what top female athletes wear. In 2018, Bloomberg reported that Eric Liedtke, an adidas board member spoke to this point, referring to adidas' female target customer he said, "[she] doesn't follow the Real Madrids, she doesn't follow the James Hardens, she follows her own cycle of influencers, and they are typically on Instagram or YouTube or the social media areas we tap into."[55]

Recognizing that women's communities are where their attention is, sports brands like adidas have changed things up. Several brands have launched ambassador programs to work with influential trainers, models, and athletes that have communities of women they interact with.

---

54 (Mau 2018)
55 (Weiss 2017)

However, this idea isn't new when it comes to connecting with women. From the '80s when the Reebok Freestyle became the popular aerobics shoe after top fitness instructors wore it in their exercise videos to Lululemon working with community yoga instructors as a means to get the word out about their brand, women's communities have been a strong source of influence. Social media has simply increased the scale, accessibility, and influence of those communities.

It all goes back to what is relatable for women's lives. While it's inspiring to see the accomplishments of women who have reached the top of their sport, it's motivating to see the fitness journeys of women facing similar scheduling and career juggling challenges but are still crushing it in the gym and meeting their fitness goals.

Interactions on social media have also changed the direction of the conversation between women and brands from one-way to two-way. Women aren't just talking to each other, they are talking with brands and giving their feedback on everything from a marketing message to products. This has shifted the power dynamic more into the hands of women. Information and the opportunity to share her opinion publicly is at every woman's fingertips

Barbara Ebersberger, VP of Performance Apparel at Reebok, summarized well how she has seen the female customer change during her tenure telling me, "Women are much more open in articulating their needs, wants, and giving feedback. Today women can buy something and then give feedback on site or social media. Even 10 years ago this wasn't possible, you just had word of mouth."

All of the brands I spoke with review all feedback and social comments as well as work to build relationships with women through social media and popular influencers in addition to traditional marketing that is less interactive. Some of the brands go so far as to revise their products, depending on the feedback they receive. Women are talking, and brands are listening.

This is why it is so important for women to use their voices. While I believe there will always be a place for women to support and encourage each other through their personal and chosen networks, I also believe that community needs to extend into sports coverage. If women want to see their favorite female athletes get more coverage and be more represented, women have an opportunity to make it happen through their increasing influence.

The 2018 *Forbes* list of the world's 100 highest-paid athletes did not include any women. Yes, you read that correctly. There wasn't one female athlete that earned enough to be on the list top paid athletes.[56] In years past one to three women have been represented, but even one to three percent is grossly disappointing.

Moreover, a study by a group of USC researchers found that ESPN's *SportsCenter* has only devoted two percent of airtime to women's sports between 1999 and 2014.[57] So, roughly two percent of women are typically on the top paid athletes list and women receive about two percent of airtime. That's an unplanned coincidence.

For those who believe that no one is interested in watching women's sports, in 2014, women represented 44 percent of NCAA athletes[58] and in the 2016 Rio Olympics, 45 percent of the competing athletes were female.[59] I'd bet those athletes, many of the women who play that sport, and their communities would be interested in watching. And, if these athletes and their sports were to receive adequate coverage, I'd also bet there would be a lot more people interested in watching.

Imagine a world where female athletes received the same level of coverage, airtime, and attention as male athletes. I'd imagine that Forbes list would look differently, more women

---

56   (Forbes 2018)
57   (Chaffee 2017)
58   Ibid
59   ("Women in Sport" 2018)

would be emulating their favorite athlete's style, and communities of female athletes would grow exponentially.

**

The key to reaching women is through their communities. Women lean on each other to provide real thoughts and recommendations for everything from athleisure brand and fitness tips to countless other questions beyond this topic. Closely tied with the rise of fitness communities, athleisure grew first through word of mouth and increasingly through social media and other online information.

No longer mere recipients of information, women are creating conversations and becoming the gatekeepers for the success of brands, influencers, and fitness trends. Brands that can connect with and become an important part of women's communities have a better chance of success. Athleisure is no exception.

More than any other time, women's voices are being heard and responded to, which gives women the opportunity to steer the creation of products, the success of brands, and the leverage to impact the change they want to see take place, particularly when it comes to all things related to sports.

FALSEHOOD 5

ONE SIZE FITS ALL

———

Traditionally, clothing sizes are based off a sample model's measurements, which are then scaled to create other sizes. This is great from an efficient manufacturing and cost perspective, but in reality, how that one model's measurements are translated to other sizes doesn't always work out for the rest of the women who are buying the clothes.

Most women, including me, have encountered the challenge of finding clothes that fit correctly. We walk into a store, find clothes we like and try them on only to end up frustrated that nothing fit. Speaking for myself, not being able to find clothes that fit has made me feel like I'm the wrong shape and size but actually, it's the clothes.

Women come in all shapes and sizes. Whether you liken our different shapes to food (pear, apple, peanut, string bean, carrot) or shapes (rectangle, inverted triangle, triangle, hourglass, rounded), we carry our weight in different areas. This means that even if you were to line up a group of women who are technically the same size, their body shapes will be different. Despite this reality, most clothes are made based on the measurements of thin and tall fit models.

As of 2017, analyst reports show that 68 percent of US women are above a size 14 but only 18 percent of clothing sold is plus size.[60] While this stat reflects the whole apparel market, not just sports related apparel, it reveals there's some ground to make up, don't you think?

When it comes to the athletic industry, the picture is much the same—a focus on a thin frame and smaller sizes. I don't know about you, but I work out five to six days a week, eat *somewhat* healthy aside from my massive sweet tooth, and I don't look like a fitness model. I do however buy a lot of clothes to work out and leisure in because I enjoy exercising and like the way athleisure fits and looks.

Athletes come in all shapes and sizes, so there needs to be clothing options for all of them. If Nike co-founder Bill

---

60   (The Economist 2017)

Bowerman's statement "If you have a body, you are an athlete" holds true, then I believe there's an opportunity to better serve athletes of all body shapes and sizes. And, you can't have athleisure without the "athletic."

Whether speaking out through social media or using their platform to break down stereotypes, women are working to change the perception that there is only one fit body type. Being fit and exercising shouldn't be limited to women of a certain size. All women should be able to enjoy the comfort and benefits of activewear, whether worn for a workout, lounging around the house, or strutting down the street to brunch.

**

We can't talk about women's sizing challenges in athleisure without mentioning the firestorm that was created after Lululemon founder Chip Wilson made a comment about women's bodies and the way leggings fit them.

In 2013, women complained that their Lululemon's Wunder Under leggings made with Luon fabric were pilling (creating little fuzzy balls in areas that rub) after little use. Given the opportunity to respond to the pilling issue during a Bloomberg interview, Chip said "Frankly some women's bodies just won't actually work for it...They don't work for some women's bodies...it's really about the rubbing through the thighs, how much pressure is there over a period of time, how much they use it."[61]

Chip's focus on women's bodies in his statement created instant backlash from women, many of whom were loyal customers that felt alienated by the very brand they had supported for years. There was significant backlash in the press and in social media about the perceived insensitive nature of his comments and the inference that larger women whose thighs were more likely to rub together could not wear Lululemon pants.

I'll go ahead and raise my hand to say that my thighs rub together. Same for most of the women I know, and if Lululemon was founded to create technically superior activewear for women, shouldn't it be a given that the clothes should be made to withstand such wear? One customer, @PinaCocoblog tweeted that she would be wearing her Lululemon "pants tonight to tennis practice and making sure my thighs rub extra, like they always do. Because I have muscles."[62]

Isn't part of being an athlete building muscle?

---

61 (Global News 2013)
62 (Huffington Post 2013)

**

Athletes come in all shapes and builds, but with as much progress as we've seen, muscular, curvy, and larger bodies still struggle with fit and acceptance.

The belief is that while it's okay for women to have some muscle, they can't be *too* muscular because that is not considered feminine. As a result, most of the athleisure options are made to fit women who are thin, despite the fact that athletes inherently build muscle through training.

This belief about women's build is residual from other limiting perceptions athletes have had to overcome. Such myths included that women are the weaker sex, that women should not participate in activities not seen as feminine like lifting weights, sweating, and being aggressive, and that participating in exercise would be detrimental to women's health.[63]

The belief that lifting weights is not seen as feminine is closely tied to the thought that women shouldn't be too muscular. Even today women are discouraged from lifting heavy weights to avoid creating bulky muscle, but instead should lift smaller weights with more repetitions.

---

63   (Wilde 2017)

Throughout my life, I've read article after article confirming or disproving this assertion. Regardless of whether it is true or false, the underlying discussion centers around how muscular women should be.

I'm a size 8 with arms that are larger than most women, so I find it a challenge to find clothes that fit me well. Having a more muscular build, most clothes are usually too tight in and around my thighs, arms, and shoulders. I can't even tell you how many shirts I've ripped or can't even try on because my arms won't fit into the arm holes. Even with my athleisure clothes, the fit on my arms is always tight. Luckily, the fabric stretches more so I'm usually able to make the fit work.

But beyond my clothes I have heard comments throughout my life about my arms from "Your arms are huge!" to "Why are your arms so big?" For years, I felt insecure about how large they were and tried to make them smaller. But, as any good fitness professional will tell you, you can't spot train and I would never stop exercising to reduce the size of my arms. Over time, I have come to appreciate my arms because they are strong and muscular.

Scrutiny is magnified for professional athletes who have to deal with comments about their body shape and size in the public eye as well as finding activewear that fits. This includes one of the greatest athletes of all time, Serena Williams.

But Serena isn't having it. In 2017 after having her daughter Alexis, Serena wrote and posted an essay on *Reddit* to her mother thanking her for remaining calm and strong over the years when so many openly commented on Serena's body.

Serena wrote, "I've been called man because I appeared outwardly strong. It has been said that that I use drugs. (No, I have always had far too much integrity to behave dishonestly in order to gain an advantage). It has been said I don't belong in Women's sports — that I belong in Men's — because I look stronger than many other women do. (No, I just work hard and I was born with this badass body and proud of it)."[64]

As a woman who remained confident despite comments on her body, Serena went on to say, "I am proud we were able to show them what some women look like. We don't all look the same. We are curvy, strong, muscular, tall, small, just to name a few, and all the same: we are women and proud!"

I believe the only suitable response to those comments is – game, set, match.

---

64 (Williams 2017)

Beyond comments, Serena has struggled to find clothes that fit as well, specifically sports bras. We've already talked about how the invention of the sports bra was critical to women's participation in sports, but even 40 years later fit is still an issue for women with larger breasts. In fact, *one in five women continues to avoid exercise because they don't have the right sports bra.*[65]

As a woman with a larger chest, Serena struggled to find a bra that worked for her on the court. According to an interview with *The CUT* in 2016, when Serena first started playing tennis she struggled to find a bra that fit her larger chest. However, after her mother recommended she check out the Australian brand Berlei while playing there, Serena has worn their bras ever since.

As of 2016, she endorses Berlei sports bras because they fit her and provide the support required for her to play like the champion she is.[66] Speaking at the Berlei U.S. launch at Macy's in 2016, Serena talked about why she has been such a oyal customer and brand advocate, saying "I've been wearing [Berlei bras] for 12 years because I have a larger bust," she said. "Some girls can play with a sheath. I need a full-on bra."[67]

---

65 (Reebok 2018)
66 (Rinkunas 2016)
67 (Barsamian 2016)

**

Changing the limiting beliefs about how female athletes should look is still a work in progress though slowly more women are using their voice to influence the change.

One of my friends who is a size 12 and works out regularly said it best when she told me, "Because of my size and the way I look, I don't really talk about how athletic I am because I don't look like a 'fit person.' But, *I am strong*, I came first place at my last spin class!"

Women are influencing change through their voice on social media. Over the years, social media has become a place of frustration and empowerment. On the one hand, many women will only post flawless photos of themselves, choosing to pose in a certain way or Photoshop out their flaws. These unrealistic images can have negative effects on other women because it sets unrealistic expectations, as *the bodies in the photo aren't real!*

There is a counter-movement of women of all shapes and sizes who are unabashedly posting authentic images of themselves. These women are showing their athleisure outfits, their muscular gains from training, and showing how they exercise among other things. In these photos, these women are proudly embracing their bodies as they are and empowering other women to do the same. Communities are being created around these women, supporting and encouraging them to be who they are and thanking them for their courage to be authentic.

Yin Liu, a woman who lives in Portland, Oregon talked with me about how she has noticed more women on Instagram and around Portland wearing body conscious outfits like crop tops with leggings. She said, "I wouldn't wear those outfits, but I'm encouraged by other women who are confident enough to do so. I can see a shift in mindset towards comfort and confidence."

Cassey Ho, a fitness influencer, is using her reach platform to help women appreciate the shape of their bodies regardless of size and change the narrative around what it means to look fit and be healthy. Cassey made a name for herself after starting a YouTube fitness channel in 2009 that expanded to fitness DVDs, books, appearances on major media outlets, and her own line of POPFLEX activewear and accessories. Her channel is now the top female fitness channel on YouTube with over 500 million video views and 4 million subscribers. In most of her posts and videos, Cassey wears athletic clothing and has undergone scrutiny about how her body looks.

In 2015, Cassey became the target of negative body shaming comments that her shape did not fit the perceived ideal for a fitness instructor. Cassey did not hesitate to speak out and created a YouTube video titled, "'Perfect' Body" that has over 12 million views and counting. In this video Cassey shows some of the mean comments that have been made about her body and then goes on to Photoshop her body in the video to achieve the shape that would meet expectations.

In an interview with *Forbes*, Cassey discussed how she and other content creators can have a positive impact on body image, stating, "YouTube is a place where creators can make content and unleash it into the online world without anyone telling us how our nose should look or how much we should weigh. We can say whatever we want to whoever will listen. It's important that girls present themselves on this platform as real and as genuine as possible because it encourages other girls to be comfortable and confident with who they are! Take the focus away from just looks and let's focus on talent, skill, and what each of us can offer to this world."[68]

＊＊

When it comes to size, women over a size 14 have even fewer athleisure options. Even Lululemon itself only offers sizes 0 to 14 as of 2018. Fewer size options means women who wear a 16 or larger are sometimes forced to get creative when

---

68   (Humphrey 2014)

heading to the gym. Their solution is similar to what I used to do when I couldn't find activewear options that fit me well in the 1990s...wear men's clothes. Given the number of options available for women size 0 to 14, this is not a solution.

"This has nothing to do with demand, and everything to do with how the society views women over a certain size," Alysse Dalessandro, independent size-inclusive founder of the personal style blog Ready To Stare and body positive advocate told *Retail Dive* in 2016. "Retailers are still seeing plus-sized consumers as an afterthought. It's not about numbers. If it were about numbers, then we'd have more options."[69]

A 2016 research study published in the *Fashion and Textiles* journal explored plus size activewear clothing for plus size women. The study found that the women in the study felt it was nearly impossible to be a larger size and dress in a feminine way. When exercising the women would resort to wearing men's clothing due to a lack of options, believing the only way to find options to wear was to lose weight.[70]

Why should women be forced to wear men's clothes to work out? Women of all sizes should have activewear options to

---

69 (Ewen 2016)
70 (Christel, O'Donnell and Bradley 2016)

wear to the gym and throughout their day that are comfortable and stylish.

Kathy Chornyak, a woman who moves between a size 18 and 20, spoke with me about how her activewear options have changed over the years. Recalling that as recently as ten years ago, when she shopped for activewear, she couldn't find women's clothes that fit her so she opted to purchase men's cotton shirts and shorts as well.

Because she couldn't ever find activewear in her size, Kathy didn't realize the benefits to wearing performance fabric. Several years ago, Kathy decided to invest more heavily in her fitness regimen and purchased her first performance shirt, a men's shirt from Lululemon.

Eventually finding that Old Navy offered activewear for women in her size, Kathy purchased more performance clothes for her workouts. Talking to me about her shopping experience, she said, "In my mind I don't think I need to shop at plus size stores until I go into a retail store and realize that I do because there aren't sizes available. I like Old Navy because they have the plus sizes in the store and it's easy. For a time, I only bought stuff online."

After being able to wear better clothes to the gym, Kathy was finally able to realize how the functional properties of activewear helped her during her workout and lasted longer than the workout clothes she had worn in the past. She loved how leggings stayed up when she worked out and prevented chaffing, allowing her to easily engage in higher intensity exercise.

Leading a healthy lifestyle is something all women should be able to engage in. Part of that lifestyle should include the ability to wear clothes that perform and make the woman wearing it feel good in the gym *and* on the street, regardless of her size.

**

Some brands are expanding women's size options through online stores or adding sizes to their lines. In 2017, Nike added plus-size t-shirts, running tights, tech hoodies, and training shorts in sizes 1XL to 3XL to its online offering.

To ensure the best fit possible, Nike designs the larger sizes based off plus-sized women. Also, instead of offering the sizes as an option on their smaller sized styles, Nike shows the larger sizes as separate styles on their site worn by women of that size.

Recognizing the importance of offering such a size range, Nike released the following statement in line with the plus-size launch, "She is an athlete, period. And having helped fuel this cultural shift, we celebrate these athletes' diversity, from ethnicity to body shape."[71] At this time most of the options are only offered online. While a step in the right direction, an online only experience limits the ability for women to shop for their size as easily as other women.

In addition to Nike, there are several other brands that offer larger sizes including Ivy Park, Torrid, ASOS, JoyLab by Target, Beyond Yoga, Old Navy Active, Athleta, Fabletics, and Outdoor Voices. Slowly more brands are being created or expanding their options to reach more women of various sizes and shapes with activewear options.

Alexandra Waldman, co-founder of Universal Standard told *Racked* in 2018 that it's "A very common misconception, that if you have a bigger body, you're not using it actively, because if you were, you wouldn't be big. It's the same as the ridiculous idea that women with bigger bodies aren't interested in fashion. It's absolute nonsense. It's completely wrong and foolish."[72]

Founded in 2015, Universal Standard is an online store that offers clothing for women ranging from activewear to

---

71   (Young 2017)
72   (Nittle 2017)

casual to more formal options. Launched with sizes 10 to 28, they recently expanding to include sizes 6 to 32 with plans to extend to offer sizes 0 to 40. All of the clothes undergo an intense process of design iterations to ensure the right style, comfort, and fit.

More than simply offering more sizes, co-founders Polina Veksler and Alexandra Waldman are redefining standard size scales with the goal to make size irrelevant and putting an end to size segregation. In addition to offering a broader range of sizes than most retailers on the market, Universal Standard is redefining what small, medium and large sizes equate to. Using the average American woman's size as a medium, Universal Standard's size scales range from a 2XS, which equates to sizes 6 to 8, a medium is 18 to 20 and a large serves women sized 22 to 24.

The reaction to the brand has been positive. "We receive so many love letters telling us how much people love what we do," Polina told *Forbes*.[73] Beyond women, the company has support of several investors, including goop's Gwyneth Paltrow, MatchesFashion founders Tom and Ruth Chapman, Toms founder Blake Mycoskie, SoulCycle's Elizabeth Cutler, and Sweetgreen's Jonathan Neman and Nicolas Jammet.

---

73 (Rabimov 2017)

With all that star power backing, it seems we are witnessing the beginning of an impactful change.

**

Women like Cassey and others who post what's real are what is going to change the narrative for good. I want to encourage even more women to not only embrace their own size and shape but also help other women to do so. A beauty standard can only persist if women allow it to. Instead of focusing on how women should look I would love to be a part of a world where women focus on how they feel, aiming to be healthy, strong, and content.

One size scale or body type does not fit all. Living a healthy lifestyle and wearing activewear shouldn't be limited to women sized 0 to 14 or of a certain shape. Women of all shapes and sizes should have the opportunity to purchase stylish and functional clothing options to enjoy the benefits of living an active lifestyle, from enduring the challenge of a hard workout to the joy of feeling comfortable throughout the day. Athleisure for *every* woman.

True athletic parity cannot happen until all athletes are provided with clothing to help them perform and look their best.

LEGGINGS ARE NOT PANTS

Okay, let's get this out of the way because we have some things to discuss. All leggings *are* pants.

According to Webster's dictionary, pants are defined as *an outer garment covering each leg separately and usually extending from the waist to the ankle.*

All leggings do in fact cover both legs and extend from the waist to the ankle...unless you are wearing cropped leggings of course. So, there you have it, *leggings are pants.*

Now that we've got that settled, let's discuss why there is such backlash against activewear leggings being worn outside of exercise as pants.

While most of this book focuses on all athleisure clothing and style, leggings have been the driving force of its rise and popularity. Even today, leggings continue to drive much of the sales for women's activewear and in turn, athleisure.

In 2016, the *Women's Wear Daily* industry publication reported that online leggings orders increased 41 percent in the previous year, compared with orders for jeans that only increased three percent during the same time.[74] While the women who purchased these leggings may not intend to wear them outside the gym, we can assume that many of them will since that's how the whole athleisure trend started in the first place.

The more women wore leggings as pants the louder the debate and discussion around their appropriateness. So naturally, we must discuss why leggings "haters" do not believe they are appropriate to be worn in public, how women are responding, and what the leggings debate is really about.

---

74   (Nahman 2016)

Like female led clothing trends of the past including any form of pant, suits, and sneakers instead of heels, leggings threaten the status quo of established norms. Whether women recognize it or not, by choosing to wear leggings amid such debate they are silently protesting those who try to restrict their choice to wear them. There's something to be said for the strength of numbers.

**

FYI, leggings are not a new addition to women's wardrobes. From Audrey Hepburn in 1957's *Funny Face* to Olivia Newton-John in 1978's *Grease* and Madonna wearing them in the 1980s, leggings have been a wardrobe option for women for decades. Heck, even I wore a uniform of black cotton stir-up leggings for a solid three years back in the 1990s.

However, while similar, activewear leggings are slightly different from their predecessors. Reasons given for why activewear leggings are not pants include the following. Leggings, or tights as they are often also called, tend to be thinner and have more stretch, lending themselves to become sheer and revealing if over-stretched.

Also, these leggings hug a woman's shape too closely in a way that can be viewed as sexualized. While the ability to see a woman's shape is helpful when reviewing form while exercising, it is less necessary outside the gym. Other reasons given in regard to leggings being worn as pants include that they are not flattering on all women and are simply too informal to be worn in public.

As the number of women wearing performance leggings, or yoga pants, outside the gym increased, so did vocal dissent. From social media videos and comments to company policies, those against leggings being worn as pants have been quite vocal about their stance.

One of the more visible statements about the appropriateness of leggings happened in 2015 when Jamie Higdon-Randolph posted a public service video on her Facebook page. Discussing how leggings should and should not be worn, the video quickly went viral, racking up over 12 million views in its first month of posting alone.

Opening the video, Jamie discusses how she loves leggings because they are comfortable, can be dressed up, and can look classy depending on how women wear them. She goes on to recommend that women make sure they don't wear leggings that are so small they become sheer and reveal what's under them.

Jamie says, "Some of you people like to use leggings as britches — as *pants* pants. That ain't how they're supposed to be worn. If you can't wear a shirt that covers your tail, so I can't tell that you got some Aztec-print thongs on, you don't need to be wearin' 'em."[75]

If women do decide to wear leggings as pants, Jamie suggests that women pair them with a longer shirt, tunic, or dress to make the outfit appropriate. But if the leggings fit correctly, why would women need to wear a longer shirt with leggings? Leggings reveal just as much of a woman's curve as skinny jeans. Why do back pockets and side rivets make that much difference?

Fashion designers like Norma Kamali, who pioneered the concept of activewear as ready-to-wear in the 1980s, believe that people are getting the leggings debate all wrong. Rather than debating their appropriateness, the focus should be on achieving the right fit.

In an interview with *The Wall Street Journal* in 2018, Norma remarked that when worn *incorrectly* "leggings [can be] even more provocative than bikinis or mini-skirts because they are worn on the street and they are closer to looking like you have second skin than any other piece of clothing."[76] How-

75 (Ritzen 2015)
76 (Malinsky and Zarrella 2018)

ever, Norma also noted that when leggings are worn *correctly* they are sleek and not shocking.

I agree with Norma, especially where fit is concerned. Like most clothing, it's all in how you wear it. When women wear leggings that fit and can bend over without revealing undergarments, the argument that leggings are sheer and therefore inappropriate to wear no longer applies.

**

Another reason leggings are not considered pants is that they outline a woman's body, booty and all, which is thought to be too revealing. To walk the line between what's comfortable and appropriate, most women wear their leggings with long tops like oversized sweaters, sweatshirts, and long shirts or dresses to cover their curves.

This rule is so widely recognized that women's activewear brand Athleta even uses the acronym "CYA," which stands for Covers Your Assets, to call out longer length casual tops that can be paired with their leggings. Such acknowledgement is a *cheeky* way to approach the issue with women as well as provide them with more conservative athleisure options.

However, some companies are not even leaving it up to women to determine how to style their leggings by taking a stance on the matter through their dress codes. In 2017, two female United passengers were kicked off a flight because they were wearing leggings. The passengers were traveling with United employee passes so were subject to the airline's employee dress code which clearly stated leggings are not considered appropriate casual attire.

The United employee travel privilege dress code states, "It's important you and your companions feel comfortable when you travel, so casual attire is allowed provided it looks neat and is in good taste for the local environment. Unacceptable pass travel attire includes beach-type rubber flip flops, slippers, anything with holes or tears, anything that reveals your midriff or undergarments and form-fitting Lycra or spandex pants, such as leggings."[77]

Some women are fighting back to change policies and the mindset around what is appropriate, including young women. In 2014, a middle school in Evanston, Illinois took such issue with leggings and banned female students from wearing them, noting they are "too distracting to boys."[78]

---

77 (Harrington and Zhang 2017)
78 (Dockterman 2014)

The female students fought back. A handful of them protested outside the school with signs that read, "Are my pants lowering your test scores?" as well as circulating a petition which 500 students signed.

Then thirteen-year-old Sophie Hasty told the Evanston Review, "For me, it's about shaming girls about their bodies," Bond said. "It's this message across genders that girls have to cover up, and teachers saying to girls, the reason for this rule is so that boys aren't distracted."[79]

On the other hand, who determines what is and isn't appropriate? Typically, the cultural norms of the time, right? Well, over half of this culture are women, so if we want to change what is and is not considered appropriate, we theoretically have the numbers to do it.

Let's remember, women wearing pants challenged the status quo for over a century, not only because they challenged male authority but also because they exposed women's ankles. Yes, ankles. In the early 1900s, exposing a woman's ankles was quite scandalous after wearing long skirts that dragged on the floor for decades.

---

79   Ibid

As hemlines inched up and corsets were discarded, women's modern fashion choices were considered risqué and shocking to those unaccustomed to seeing women wear unstructured and shorter dresses. Adding to the perceived *vulgarity*, arm sleeves were shortened and necklines slightly lowered.[80]

Changes to women's clothing and the resulting body exposure was considered so shocking that government regulations were actually enforced to minimize the amount of leg, arm, and necklines uncovered. More than a simple ban, in some parts of the U.S. during the 1920s women were actually *fined* or *arrested* if their skirts were shorter than the regulated length. Some areas required skirts longer than four inches below the knee or no higher than three inches above the ankle.[81]

Nearly a hundred years later American women not only wear much shorter skirts, but they also wear shorts and tank tops freely without hesitation or resistance. So, while it may seem risqué today that leggings show the outline of a woman's figure, I'll predict this will lessen over time to where it's not even discussed any longer.

---

80 (Koo-Seen-Lin 2013)
81 (Lee 2003)

First, at least women aren't being arrested for wearing leggings in public without covering their bottoms, so we are already ahead there. Second, this argument seems like semantics to me. Why is it okay to wear leggings without a long top in the gym but not outside of the gym? Because that is what we've been told and accepted as true, *but* we can and are changing what is considered acceptable. History has proven that is possible.

**

One of the remaining arguments against women wearing leggings as pants is that not all women look good in them. This point really gets to the root of a belief that the shape and size of a woman dictates what she can and cannot wear. To this I say, no more. Cultural beauty standards are arbitrary and I'm done allowing myself and other women to be defined by them. Regardless of what a woman looks like, she can rock leggings if she chooses.

While only a piece of a much larger body positive movement was discussed earlier, what has happened with leggings is representative of a bigger movement towards body inclusivity. In making the decision to wear clothing that emphasizes their curves, women are symbolically telling others, "I embrace how my body is shaped."

There's something very empowering about accepting your body for the way it is and not hiding your shape behind layers of clothing. I've experienced this for myself. Over the last few years I've worked to embrace my own unique curves after spending so many years trying to change or hide them.

The thing about leggings is that if you're going to wear them, you've gotta commit to the way they fit. Yes, they will lift and tuck you in some areas, but there's only so much reshaping a garment can do. And, even if I cover my bottom, leggings will still show the shape of my legs.

Once I started wearing leggings to the gym every day I got used to seeing my shape and how it changed with my workouts. Now when I put on leggings I feel empowered because I don't even think about my shape because I've already owned it, day in and day out.

The more women are encouraged to embrace their own shape, the more women will wear what they want, and not what they think they should wear, including leggings outside the gym. The more women of different shapes and sizes wear leggings, the more the beauty standards will change.

**

With any change to women's wardrobes, there is an initial backlash but eventually the change becomes the norm. I believe that we are over the hump when it comes to the initial objections to women wearing leggings.

As athleisure has evolved over the last few years and the public has become more used to seeing women wearing leggings, the stigma associated with wearing them has quieted slightly. However, there are still limitations to when, where, who, and how women can wear leggings outside of a fitness setting. But if history is any indicator, as leggings become even more mainstream and part of everyday outfits, the "leggings haters" will move on to focus on a new "inappropriate" piece of clothing soon enough.

When it comes to what clothing is considered appropriate, women have the power to change the rules. On a small scale, women can continue to wear leggings whenever and wherever they want. On a larger scale, they can fight policies and make their voices heard about the restrictions placed on their clothes. Some have even launched their own brand that offers even more women with athleisure options, which we will discuss in a later chapter.

Also, in my opinion, the benefit of leggings goes far beyond the comfort and mobility they provide. Leggings are more than pants; they empower women to embrace their own shape and size. I don't think it's any coincidence that most superhero uniforms include some form of leggings as part of a body suit. There's something about wearing athletic clothing that makes you feel like you can take on both a workout and the world.

FALSEHOOD 7

ATHLEISURE IS LAZY

As of 2018, athleisure is a $44 billion dollar industry in the U.S. That happened because athleisure has become the way more women dress to fit their lifestyle. While there will always be a place for athletic clothes worn for working out, the leisure aspect of athleisure is what many women choose to wear the rest of the day.

However, even though women are choosing comfort that doesn't mean they are putting less effort into their appearance. With all of the fashionable options women have today, athleisure outfits are anything but lazy; they are part of the modern woman's wardrobe.

It's the 21st century and women need clothes that work with their lifestyle. Women juggle their jobs, family, fitness, friends, personal commitments and more. Changing clothes for each part of the day is a hassle. With such crazy busy days, women need clothes that are stylish, versatile, machine washable, and *comfortable*. Whether it's dry shampoo or leggings, anything that makes women's lives easier can quickly become a necessity.

Because athleisure is versatile, women are choosing to wear it throughout their week from work, to working out, and weekend activities. With more options to choose from it's easier for women to style their athleisure outfits in ways that help them go from the office to the bar and have a more active day.

Athleisure isn't just for the weekends anymore, it's a new casual option for every day.

**

In my experience, most women will tell you they love athleisure because it's comfortable, among other reasons. But what does that really mean?

Well I'll tell you what it doesn't mean, and that's sloppy. Yes, I realize you may be thinking about those huge sweatpants or worn-in leggings that nearly every woman has had for years and puts on to binge watch the latest season of their new favorite show. That's not what I'm talking about. That ritual is sacred and those pants only leave the house under a dire emergency. What I'm talking about are the clothes women leave the house wearing.

Comfort is about how the fit of clothes makes women feel. Part of that is literal, the clothes tend to have more stretch, so no matter how a woman's body looks that day the clothes are still likely to fit, and that is comforting. When it comes to athleisure, women don't have to spend as much time thinking through what pieces of her closet fit and look good together. Instead, athleisure is a matter of putting on a pair of leggings (high-waisted are the best) and pair it with a jacket or sweatshirt and go.

The other part is that more of the athleisure options are stylish and can be put together in a way that reflects a woman's personal style. Some women, like me, enjoy wearing a sportier look. The combination of feeling good and looking good is powerful. The stretch and style that athleisure provides makes it that much easier for women to get dressed, feel good about what they are wearing because it's still stylish, and get on with the day.

Katie Warner Johnson, co-founder of the online luxury activewear retailer Carbon38, pretty much nails it when she told the *Fashion Week Daily* in July 2018, "It feels simple to put on a pair of leggings, but it's so powerful because there's freedom in that decision. There's freedom in not having to button a pair of jeans around our bellies after a meal. There's so much power in being able to slip something on that makes you feel sexy and supported, and you can throw it in the machine if you drop something on it because you're running about your day. Athleisure is no longer this joke of like, 'I'm wearing my workout clothes to brunch.' It's like, 'Damn straight, I'm wearing my leggings and they look amazing.' I haven't bought a pair of jeans in years!"[82]

More casual and comfortable doesn't necessarily mean less effort. Where the go-to casual outfit may have been jeans and a t-shirt or sweater in the past, now that includes some form of leggings and an oversized sweater or other combinations. I consider this a style choice getting dressed just the same, and not exerting any less effort. Since we've agreed that leggings are pants, if women put on leggings they are therefore getting dressed.

Marshal Cohen, chief industry analyst of The NPD Group, Inc. talked about whether the casualization of clothing is going to last stating, "I'm often asked if the athleisure trend is going to fade away, and the answer is no. When you have

---

82 ("Carbon38's Katie Warner Johnson On the Deeper Significance Of Athleisure" 2018)

comfort and function combined with fashion, it's difficult to go back to anything else on a regular basis."[83]

To help understand what women really mean when they say they wear athleisure because it's comfortable, I asked them. As I found, comfort means not having to think about the fit of your clothes or the restrictions they may cause. Importantly, despite the desire to be comfortable, women were not often willing to compromise style to a point where they felt unpresentable.

Jacky Fonantella, a woman who loves to wear leggings often, especially when she works from home told me, "Comfort is when you don't notice what you're wearing and don't have to adjust your clothes when they're on. Nothing is digging into me and I don't feel constricted." At the same time, Jacky was quick to reinforce that she also doesn't "want to look schlubby" and that it's important to still look fashionable even when she's comfortable.

Similarly, Casey Lance, a woman who wears athleisure while traveling and on the weekends, said, "Comfort is a lot about fit and function. I hate it when my pants are too tight, which is a bonus for athleisure because the clothes are more forgiving, flexible, and move with you more than other pants.

83　(The NPD Group, Inc. 2018)

I don't like to feel constricted." Casey also quickly followed by telling me that it's also important to be stylish, distinguishing between different types of athleisure. "I choose my gym clothes for function, but choose my athleisure wear based on style," she said.

Women's decision to choose clothes that make them feel good is what comfort is all about. Clothes have a powerful effect on the person wearing them, and the combo of stylish comfort is one that is driving the decision to wear more athleisure.

In addition, athletic brands like Reebok are recognizing this is how women are wearing their clothes more and more. As Barbara Ebersberger, VP of Performance Apparel at Reebok told me about how she and her team are thinking about their women's apparel, "I would love to create products that customers wouldn't even have to think about how to wear it because the clothes are seamlessly integrated into their personal lives. The clothes should adapt to their busy lifestyle no matter what they are doing. So, everything we are doing that is performance based is with the mindfulness that the product can potentially look good outside of the gym. And, no one wants to wear something that doesn't look good in the first place."

**

When it comes to the "leisure" side of athleisure there are many options and styles to choose from to mix and match. Beyond the ever so famous leggings, there are joggers, which are loose fitting tailored pants made of various fabrics from technical to sweatshirt material, as well as track pants. For tops, there are various sweatshirts, jackets, sweaters, cardigans, and shirts to name a few.

For each of these options there are many, many, *many* style, fabrication, silhouette and design options, brands, and price points from which to choose. So, while athleisure may be the new uniform, each woman can easily express her own personal style. Depending on a woman's personal style, she can create an athleisure look that is preppy, urban, relaxed, sporty, or a mix of each.

My wardrobe has a little bit of everything. I'd describe my own style as a mix of sporty and chic. I love finding a pair of leggings made with some added details like side zipper pockets or a sweatshirt with an interesting design detail to take things up a notch to make me feel stylish.

Joggers are an important part of my wardrobe because they have the stretch and comfort of leggings but aren't as tight so are perfect to pair with shorter tops. No "CYA" necessary. If you don't have a pair yet, I highly recommend trying them out. In my opinion, they are updated sweatpants because they are tailored, so they look chic but are still comfortable.

I enjoy pairing both joggers and leggings with various long shirts, track jackets, sweaters, and sweatshirts of every kind – cropped, hooded, zip, and more. And, of course most of my outfits are paired with sneakers of all brands and styles, from classic to new.

While this wardrobe hasn't seen the inside of a gym, I still consider it athleisure because the clothes are often made with the same fabric used for activewear and have a sporty look, so wearing these clothes encourages a more active day, including spontaneous walks.

So, why do women have two athleisure wardrobes, the first being what they wear to the gym and possibly somewhere before or afterwards, and the other being purchased specifically for leisure? Two reasons—First, women are concerned with the gym perfume their workout clothes may acquire over time through exercise use.

Second, they appreciate the thicker material and styling of the more fashionable and leisure focused options for casual use but don't provide the level of support needed for working out. Also, thicker fabric does not reveal a woman's natural imperfections, making her more confident to wear the clothes in public.

Shelby Hall, a woman who lives in Washington, D.C. and wears athleisure to work, on the weekends to go out in and after a workout, differentiates her athletic options from her leisure ones by fabric and style. Shelby told me, "I pick out clothes to either go with heels or buy it for running, not both. There's a distinct difference between the two in my eyes."

Talking about the differences between leggings, she explained, "For running tights I look for features like a pocket with a zipper for my phone and support. I don't like to wear workout leggings to work because they're shiny." Differentiating further between workout and leisure leggings she said, "For fashion leggings I'm spending money on the trend instead of features. The leggings I wear with heels or for fun are trendy and thicker than my running tights."

Shelby's athleisure wardrobe doesn't stop with activewear leggings. "I have a lot of trendy options like joggers or drop crotch pants. Because I can get the same thing at a sports apparel company as other retailers, I have more choices in terms of quality and design when I shop."

Alternatively, for other women, the difference between wearing straight activewear outside of the gym and creating more street friendly looks is the addition of another piece of clothing that looks more casual.

Amy Waugh, a personal trainer who lives in Columbus, Ohio, described how she styles her outfits to take her from a training session to other appointments in her day. "It has a lot to do with your third layering piece or how you're accessorizing the outfit. You can be wearing a shirt and leggings at the gym but if you put a leather jacket, wrap, scarf, or cardigan it makes a big difference."

Not to leave out sneaker talk, Amy told me, "Shoes are also important. I have workout shoes and then my sneakers that I don't work out in but they are my athleisure shoes that are neutral and more fashionable and make the outfit look put together."

Amy said it. Many times, it all comes down to how women style their athleisure, and a third piece helps to transition the outfit from one environment to another. Mixing casual clothes, street clothes, active clothes, or any other type of clothes creates outfits that are easy to take from the gym elsewhere and is what makes athleisure so versatile. Beyond the clothes, how a woman accessorizes also makes a difference and helps women create a look all their own, just like any other fashion outfit.

Swapping out sneakers altogether with heels and adding a jacket can take leggings from day to night very quickly. While heels aren't exactly the most comfortable, the versatility of the rest of the athleisure-ly outfit makes it easy for any woman to keep her schedule going without major wardrobe changes. Less hassle means being able to focus on the day that much more.

∗∗

The versatility of athleisure extends into the workplace. More companies recognize the distinction between dressing comfortably and looking disheveled, deciding to allow athleisure as part of their casual dress code.

Mariana DiMartino, SVP at Turner, a public relations agency in New York City talked to *The New York Post* in 2017 about the difference between casual and sloppy. "We're a casual office, but you won't find associates running around in ill-fitting sweatpants," she explained. "Athleisure is about versatility and pairing . . . high and low aesthetics. It's polished, creative and versatile."[84]

I have found this to be true of my current casual work environment. Even though I wear some form of athleisure every

---

84 (Salemi 2016)

day, mixing casual, street, and more formal clothes with activewear pieces, I have found that my co-workers still consider my outfits professional enough for a casual work environment.

I still look pulled together because I have been thoughtful about how "straight from the gym" my outfits look. I put the same amount of effort into my hair and make-up as I used to when I worked in a business casual environment, none of my clothes looks worn, and all of them fit me appropriately for the workplace.

On a side note about clothes looking worn, athletic clothes are so much easier to care for than other clothes. Dry cleaning and ironing is not required, which is *such* a time and money saver. All I have to do is wash the clothes and hang dry them and they look as good as new. The more clothes I can buy that are this low maintenance the better.

Wearing athletic clothes to the office is just the latest addition to the casualization of the workplace. Slowly we've moved from suits, to chinos, to jeans and now to athleisure. Remember when casual Fridays was a big step? Now wearing chinos and jeans is a lot more commonplace every day of the week, despite initial criticism that dressing down at work was the downfall of all that is proper.

In the book, *The End of Fashion,* author Teri Agins discusses how, throughout the 20th century, American style became increasingly casual and customer driven. In her book, Teri wrote about the reaction to the shift towards a more casual wardrobe, writing, "It seemed as though not only dress-up clothes, but good taste, had fallen by the wayside as millions of Americans sank into sloppiness, wedded to their fanny packs, t-shirts, jeans, and chunky athletic shoes."[85]

She goes on to reference the cover headline of *Newsweek* from February 20, 1995, which read, "Have We Become a Nation of Slobs?" which discussed evidence that "people were no longer dressing to impress." This shift is most evident in Silicon Valley where male business leaders like Mark Zuckerberg wear a uniform that includes some form of shirt, jeans, and sneakers. While male leaders are often noted as driving the shift to more casual dress, I think it's only a matter of time before a prominent female business leader will be sporting her own casual work uniform, which may be athleisure.

With leggings in the picture, jeans are now considered the dressy alternative to leggings. This shift towards more relaxed dress codes has only increased since 1995. According to a Society for Human Resources Management 2018 Employee Benefits Survey, 62 percent of organizations allow

---

85   (Agins 2001)

casual dress only once a week while 50 percent allow it every day, an 18 percent increase since 2014.[86]

The reason athleisure, and more specifically leggings work so well in the workplace, is that they can be dressed up or down. "Leggings are more of a "utility" item: Some women might be wearing them for workouts or as pajamas, while others might be wearing them to the office. Leggings, these days, have more use uses than jeans," as Jaimee Minney, VP of Marketing at Slice Intelligence, an e-commerce analytics firm told *The Washington Post* in 2016.[87]

Rachel Nemceck, who works for a professional sports team, told me, "If I can get away with it and look presentable and put together, I will always rather be in some form of athleisure." This means that some creativity is required to get away with wearing leggings to work and still look professional.

When wearing leggings to work, Rachel will pair her leggings with long sweaters to ensure her bottom is covered and boots instead of sneakers to dress up her outfit. Whether she is dressing for work or heading out with friends on the weekend, Rachel is conscious about the image she projects based on her outfit. At work she feels it is important for her

---

86 ("2018 Employee Benefits: The Evolution of Benefits" 2018)
87 (Halzack 2016)

to look presentable and pulled together to be taken seriously as a professional.

This versatility makes it easy to go from the office to an event after work to the gym, making women's lives easier because they can set their outfit for the day, bring an extra third piece to help the outfit transition from day to night and go. Less need to change, less hassle, and fewer clothes to have to deal with. Layer on the fact that wearing comfortable clothes at work makes some of us (I'm raising my hand) more productive because we are focused on our work instead of our clothes, and you've got a good case for why women are wearing athleisure more.

Shaw-chin Chiu is a woman who creatively works athleisure into her office outfits, not only for comfort but also to help her maintain her active lifestyle. Living in San Diego, California, Shaw-chin works as a consultant and follows a consistent workout regimen. With her demanding schedule, Shaw-chin thinks of creative ways to fit everything in through her wardrobe decisions.

Because fitness is an important part of Shaw-chin's life, making time to exercise is a priority. Being a consultant also means she is often traveling for work, requiring she pack clothes for the office and gym, which can easily stack up. To combat this challenge, Shaw-chin will try to reduce the number of clothes she has to pack by wearing activewear pieces at work to easily transition to the gym.

Depending on the client she is currently working with and the formality of their office environment, Shaw-chin will incorporate more or less activewear into her outfit. For instance, when working for a client with a more casual work environment, she would wear a workout top under her suit jacket (her third piece) as a camisole paired with black leggings and knee-high boots. As another time hack, Shaw-chin would run the stairs of the office high-rise building when she had to work later than usual.

Shaw-chin told me, "Working with luxury retailers as clients requires that I maintain a certain level of stylishness; however, my job requires to be on a constant move between meetings and client sites. These special leggings allow me to move comfortably with style." Ever the athlete, Shaw-chin refers to the action of wearing activewear outside the gym as "flexing" her clothes to do more.

Like most other women I spoke with, Shaw-chin purchases different activewear for the gym and work, even though she will wear her work leggings to work out in when necessary. While she chooses to purchase most of her workout activewear at a discount, she will spend more money on her work leggings to ensure they do not look like activewear. She also reserves those nicer office leggings for gym "date nights" with her husband.

For women who work from home or for themselves, the dress code becomes even easier. One of these women is Cathy Zhang who lives in Oregon and runs her own watercolor design company. Currently, Cathy mixes up where she chooses to work from, bouncing from her home to coffee shops depending on the day.

Talking to me about what she chooses to wear, Cathy told me, "I wear athleisure every day if not from top to bottom. I will also mix things up, wearing leggings with a normal top or a workout tank with skinny jeans because workout tanks look just like normal tanks." Cathy also noted that living in Portland, Oregon also influences her inclination to wear athleisure because almost everyone looks like they are headed to or just came from the gym.

Discussing why she chooses to wear athleisure Cathy said, "Our body changes as we get older, so comfort is important in addition to being casual and stylish. Athleisure combines style and comfort, especially among women in their mid-30s."

Whether working in an office or from home, the casualization of the workplace has provided women with the opportunity to choose clothing they prefer to wear, and sometimes that is athleisure. Whether they are buying athleisure specifically for work or wearing their gym activewear to work, women are choosing what athleisure they wear when based on how they need it to work for them throughout their day.

**

Beyond style and comfort, athleisure often leads to more movement, as you'd expect athletic clothing to do. If clothes are easy to wear and aren't restrictive, that's one less thing to worry about that day. How is wearing athletic clothing lazy if it encourages movement?

For me, wearing my athleisure means I'm more likely to take the stairs, park farther away from destination than I need to get a walk in, use my standing desk at work, and *sometimes* walk the longer path to where I need to go...unless I'm late. I make more active choices consistently throughout my day because I'm wearing comfortable clothes that don't restrict me in any way.

A woman who makes a focused effort on keeping her activity up throughout the day is Arlie Yruma, a working mother of two. Beyond attending spin classes or going for a run when her schedule allows, Arlie always pushes herself to walk

10,000 steps a day, tracking each and every step with her Fitbit.

Arlie believes she is able to walk so much throughout the day because of the clothes she wears to the office and on weekends, which often includes a piece of activewear and flat shoes, sometimes sneakers, that allow her to walk as much as possible. At work, she will try to wear clothes that look like traditional casual wear but are made with performance fabric, while at the gym she chooses workout activewear that motivates her to push her limits.

When I asked Arlie what athleisure means to her, she told me, "Having the freedom to move with my day from moving around at work to running after my kids at soccer practice. Creating an outfit that is able to keep up with my life."

In situations where she may be the only one wearing athleisure like at a child's birthday party, Arlie is unfazed. She told me, "Because I'm wearing athleisure I get to roll around with the kids at the birthday party, helping them swing and do back flips. That's why athleisure is part of my wardrobe; it allows me to be part of the action instead of sitting on the sidelines."

This same sentiment was echoed by other mothers who also choose to wear athleisure as a way to help them be more active with their kids but still look pulled together for casual activities. Sometimes exercise isn't limited to working out; sometimes it's spending a day chasing after kids, picking up the house, and walking the dog. All of which is easier with stretchy clothes that are comfortable.

**

Athleisure isn't just for coffee after the gym anymore, it's becoming the way women dress throughout their day in different ways. Women have demanding schedules, so having clothes that easily transition to different events in the same day, allowing for more movement throughout the day, and taking their mind off their clothes and onto their jobs or current task is going to get attention.

Just because women are wearing comfortable clothes doesn't mean they are giving any less thought to how they look. It's all about how outfits are styled, and how with the many options women have between top athletic apparel companies and other brands offering fashionable athletic options, mixing and matching casual and athletic clothing can create comfortable, versatile, and chic outfits.

Women's decision to wear athleisure isn't about giving up on getting dressed for the day, it's about them making a decision to wear clothes that work for their lives and situation.

FALSEHOOD 8

"SHRINK IT AND PINK IT" WORKS

———

Let's just get this out of the way. The connection between pink and women is arbitrary. Until the mid-19th century, babies were welcomed with white clothing and accessories. Around that time, pink and blue were added to the baby color palette. In 1918, a department store declared that pink was for boys, blue for girls because pink was considered a *stronger* color, blue more *delicate*. This was reversed in the 1940s based on how manufacturers and retailers decided to assign the colors by gender.[88]

---

88   (Wilson 2013)

So basically, one day someone decided that pink was for girls and blue for boys and henceforth everything made for girls is pink and for boys is blue. But what about girls who prefer blue or boys who prefer pink? Why is gender still assigned a color?

Color options offered based on gender has to stop. Gender doesn't dictate color preferences. The assumption that a product will appeal to women if it is pink is limiting to both women and men. Yes, a lot of women like the color pink but they also appreciate other colors, so to only offer women a pink option is limiting.

Sometimes women will pick the pink color when offered other options, but other times women simply want the same item made for men but sized appropriately. *The best way to know what women want is to ask them* and not assume all women want the same thing.

What does this color rant have to do with athleisure? Well up until recently, most athletic apparel companies took a "men's first" design approach. Women's products were often made smaller and colored "pink" to appeal to women rather than designing products for women, referred to as "shrink it and pink it." Beyond the color pink, either assumptions were made about what women want or women's products received far less attention than men's products.

As we've already discussed, it took a lot of time for female-focused products to be created from the first sports bra to the first pair of athletic sneakers and even female first designed activewear. This is changing as more brands realize that women's products shouldn't be an afterthought and assumptions about what women want are limiting for both the brand and female customers.

Sometimes women don't want a different product while other times it's important to cater products and messaging to women's specific needs and challenges. An important component to landing this distinction is including more women in the decision-making from leadership to product design.

**

If you hadn't guessed already, I am not fond of the color pink. However, that doesn't mean that I don't support other women wearing it, it's a fun color! I just prefer a wardrobe of black, grey, and navy, which most of my friends think is boring, but I love.

When I used to shop for athletic sneakers to wear in the 1990s and early 2000s I had a heck of a time choosing between the overwhelming selection of white, pink, and other pastel colored women's options. The other option I had was to buy a men's sneaker if I wanted to find a color combination that

I actually liked. This meant I was selecting a shoe based on color and style instead of performance because I couldn't bring myself to wear a shoe color I disliked.

I'd ask the store associates why all the sneakers were in pastel colors and if they sold the response would be something like "you'd be surprised, women really like the pink sneakers and buy them." I'd walk away from that conversation muttering under my breath asking myself who these women were and why I can't get a *darn* sneaker in the same colors and styles offered for men.

More than color, I usually liked the men's styles a lot more. The women's styles looked dated to me while the men's styles were updated regularly with new designs. Men's styles would be featured in the store windows and have these amazing displays. By comparison, women's shoe options were limited to a few styles on the shelves in the back of the store. It was extremely frustrating and insulting. Why didn't women's shoes get the same amount of attention?

What I've come to realize from my own experience is that when women are given a limited number of colors or only pink as a choice there are three likely results. First, some women do genuinely like the pink options and purchase them with excitement. These are likely the women to whom the sales associates were referring. Second, they can be purchased out of necessity for lack of better options. Or, third, women can choose to not make a purchase. Only a third of these options ends with a happy outcome.

In an interview with *The Washington Post*, Marti Barletta, author of *"Marketing to Women"* explains, "Where manufacturers really go wrong is when they assume that if they make something pink, women will buy it. Like when an item comes in only two colors, black and pink. Or when sports apparel in women's sizes is made only in pastels. When pink is a color women can choose, they will choose it. When it is the only color that isn't the 'normal' one, women will not choose it. They don't want it forced on them."[89]

Women's products deserve the same amount of attention as men's products. It's not enough to resize a men's style for women, make it pink, and call it a day. It's important to think through how women will be using the shoe, who will likely be buying it and what she is looking for, same as men. Sometimes women want function, sometimes fashion and sometimes something in between.

Discarding the notion that pink is *the* requirement to sell to women and focusing on what women want from a product's design has led to greater success for many brands. Because,

---

89 (Contera 2016)

at the end of the day, the issue isn't about the color, it is about the lack of proper attention given to products for women and female athletes.

**

"Most of the things marketers do don't have to have a gender," Jim Winters, president of branding agency Badger & Winters told *The Washington Post* in 2016 in reference to how marketers have missed the mark with women. *"Women are not a special-interest group. They are over half the population."*[90]

Not choosing to give women's products the proper attention they deserve is leaving a lot of money on the table, as they say in business. Women make up half of the U.S. population but impact between 70 to 80 percent of consumer purchases as the primary caregiver in households, totaling nearly $18 trillion in 2018.[91] Moreover, according to reports, U.S. women control $14 trillion in assets or roughly 51 percent of personal wealth. This number is expected to climb to $22 trillion by 2020.[92]

So the question remains, how did it get to a point where women's buying power had gotten so large and yet marketing

90 Ibid
91 (King 2017)
92 (BMO Financial Group 2015)

and products were failing to connect with women's wants and needs?

Two things. First, the "shrink it and pink it" strategy was a common strategy believed to be successful. And second, most of the decision makers were men who didn't consult women as part of the design or decision-making process.

An organization that learned the benefits of moving beyond the pink strategy is the NFL. As of 2011, women made up 44 percent of the NFL's 79 million fans, according to NFL VP of Consumer Products, Tracey Bleczinski.[93] Efforts to reach women in the early 2000s consisted of offering women smaller, pinker, and sparklier versions of men's jerseys, resonating with some women...but not as many as they *could* be connecting to.

Shifting gears, the NFL launched the "Fit For You" campaign in 2011, offering fashionable and sporty fitted jerseys for women in NFL *team* colors. This new campaign grew the NFL's women's business "by a factor of 21 since 2001," up 40 percent alone in early season sales in 2011, according to Joanna Hunter, Manager of Corporate Communications for the NFL.[94]

---

93   (Baskin 2011)
94   Ibid

These results show that yes, some women do like the pink option, but other women want jerseys in team colors styled for them. Looks like a touchdown to me!

The NFL wasn't the only sports brand or organization to place less of an emphasis on women's products. As discussed in previous chapters, Title IX changed women's participation in sports. Prior to 1972, women's participation in sports was low, making it difficult to warrant much focus.

Many of the top athletic brands known today were founded before Title IX was passed and were founded with a focus on men's apparel and footwear that continued for years, even after launching women's.

Dassler Brothers Shoe Factory was founded by Rudolf "Rudi" Dassler and Adolf Dassler in 1924 until the brothers split and Rudi created Puma in 1948 and Adolf Dassler created adidas in 1949. Neither brand makes public note of when they began offering women's apparel and footwear. Nike was founded by Phil Knight and Bill Bowerman in 1964, launching Nike Women in 1978. Under Armour was founded after Title IX in 1996 and launched UA Women in 2003.

Despite the growing number of women participating in sports after 1972, sports apparel and footwear companies continued to focus largely on men's products, dedicating fewer resources to the design of women's products and/or "shrinking and pinking" men's.

While low sports participation among women may not have warranted a lot of focus by top sports brands around at the time, the growth rate of that participation seemed to go unnoticed. The male dominated leadership at many of these and other sports brands and retailers continued dedicating most resources and retail floor space to men's apparel and footwear. Female athletes and even women who wanted to wear sportswear had limited options that did not always fit their needs.

Matt Powell, VP and Senior Industry Advisor for The NPD Group, Inc. told *The Washington Post* in 2014 that women have "been vastly underserved by the industry. Sporting goods is a guy industry, and men dominate the executive ranks." Explaining further Matt said, "Even today we don't see brands making a ton of women's sporting apparel. With footwear, for example, they still tend to be female versions of a man's shoe."[95]

The industry focus on menswear left a huge opportunity for female focused brands like Lululemon, Athleta, Sweaty Betty and others to make an impact. And, once these brands

---

95   (Harwell 2014)

showed there was an opportunity, more brands emerged and influenced how top athletic brands approached their women's products.

To provide women with products they want to buy and wear, it's important to have women involved in the design process as well as part of the leaders making decisions.

The laser focus not only on the technical aspects of the fabric but also on what women think and want are key factors that contribute to a loyal following.

Speaking of alternatives, adidas, Under Armour, and Nike have each begun focusing even more effort on their women's products and marketing, showing they understand what female athletes want and need. Much of this effort has involved adding women to their leadership teams and as designers and consultants to the product design process.

ADIDAS

On the heels of its successful collaboration with Yohji Yamamoto, adidas launched a collection with designer Stella McCartney in 2005. For women's athletic apparel, this was the first that merged fashion and function. When asked by *Glamour* magazine in 2013 what drew her to activewear, Stella said, "I really felt women were getting the tail end of the design in active wear; not getting the technology or design we deserved. It was reserved for men. We were getting the leftover work from the sports design houses; I felt our colors were always baby pinks and pony blues, and I found it slightly insulting as a woman."[96]

Getting more specific about why designing more stylish options was important to her, Stella told *Glamour,* "I didn't want to feel ashamed when walking to the gym if I bumped into a friend of mine; I wanted to feel good about the way I looked. I didn't understand why style had to be sacrificed for sports technology."

At the time, this collaboration was a risk. No other top sports apparel brand had focused on providing women with fashionable sportswear. As Stella said, most of the design focus for activewear had been reserved for men, so focusing on the design for women was overdue. The success of this partnership is evident as fourteen years later, the adidas and Stella McCartney collaboration is still releasing new collections.

While the Stella McCartney collaboration was certainly a step in the right direction, the rest of the adidas women's apparel line also needed a greater design focus. Committing to an even stronger focus on their women's products, adidas

---

96 (Malinsky 2013)

brought on Christine Day in 2016 as a consultant to review their core women's sportswear strategy. She had previously worked as the chief executive officer for Lululemon, stepping down from her role in 2013.

Describing why adidas approached Christine, Nicole Vollebregt, a 20-year adidas veteran that is the brand's first global head of adidas's women's business, stated in a press release, "Christine definitely shares our vision. We see the potential in athletic women leading multidimensional lives fueled by sport and nutrition."[97]

In that same year, adidas launched the PureBoost X, a running shoe designed for women based on three years of research and testing with athletes after recognizing that women's feet react differently while running. As stylish as it was functional, the PureBoost X was the first to have a floating arch that provides support that also adapts to different foot shapes, sizes, and strikes.

"Traditionally, running shoes have been men's shoes that have been adapted for women's needs," said Jennifer Thomas, adidas's senior director for global running brands. "This all started with feedback, which was that what they really

---

97   (Kish 2014)

wanted in a performance running shoe was total innovation and total style without compromising on each of those."

From female focused design collaborations to sneakers, adidas has certainly upped its women's apparel and footwear game and shed the men's first approach.

UNDER ARMOUR

Launching its first women's line in 2001, Kevin Plank, CEO and founder of Under Armour talked to *WWD*, a fashion industry publication, in 2014 about the company's first failed attempt at creating a women's line that ended with $600,000 of clothes in an incinerator. He said, "shrink it and pink it doesn't work. We learned that nine men sitting around a table can't create product for women."[98]

Despite this insight, similar to other sports brands, UA continued to be largely male led and focused. In 2012, Kevin brought on Leanne Fremar, who had previously worked at Theory as the executive creative director for its women's business. Leanne hired even more women, including Heidi Sandreuter from PepsiCo, to be the VP of Women's Marketing.

---

98   (Palmieri 2014)

In 2014, Heidi helped launched a women's focused marketing campaign, "I Will What I Want." The campaign focused on stories of several female athletes, including American Ballet Theatre principal dancer Misty Copeland and supermodel Gisele Bündchen, who overcame challenges to rise above the limitations others placed on them in pursuit of their goals.

During an AdWeek behind-the-scenes interview, Heidi discussed the decision to choose a relatively unknown ballerina to lead the campaign over a well-known athlete. She said it was admittedly a "disruptive choice" that shows a change in the type of athlete UA wants to sponsor. "It speaks to how we're trying to incorporate more women into the fold," she said.[99] The brand was shifting its focus to reach more athletic females, not just professional athletes.

The campaign struck a chord with women, going viral across the internet and helping Under Armour become a more significant player for women's athletic apparel.

However, despite the female focused marketing, UA's apparel design remained focused on the technical aspects of product design over style. Recognizing this, Under Armour began making even more investments in the aesthetics of its women's apparel.

---

99   (Mccarthy 2014)

In 2017, Kevin told analysts, "We need to become more fashion. The consumer wants it all. That consumer may still sometimes work out like a jock—but he (or she) wants to look good doing it."[100]

This greater focus on fashion led UA to co-design and launch the Misty Copeland Signature Collection with the principal dancer in early 2018. While performance based, the line was beautifully designed with a clear focus on fashion.

Describing the line, Misty stated in a press release, "I wanted a line where we could feel fierce in the gym, and at the same time, feel confident wearing the same look out to dinner, running errands or living our everyday lives."[101]

Towards the end of 2018, UA shifted its focus once more. While still committed to style, Under Armour stepped back from fashion a bit, deciding to renew its focus on clothing designed for *athletes* in late 2018.

In an interview with the *Financial Times* in December, Kevin talked about the importance of performance for UA saying, "If they [consumers] want to go sit on the couch they can, but that product was built to help them get through a 10-mile

---

100 (Bain 2017)
101 (Under Armour 2018)

run." He went on to say, "We are a performance brand. That is what we're going to be and going to stand for, becoming the best in the world at that."[102]

Regardless of what the product looks like, UA continues to be focused on improving its women's products and messaging. In the same interview, Kevin also mentioned efforts to continue increasing the number of women in leadership positions.

NIKE

Nike has also become more focused on its women's products. Beyond launching larger size options mentioned in an earlier discussion, Nike has also focused on expanding its athletic and casual sneaker options for women.

As already mentioned, most athletic sneakers were made for men and retrofitted for women. Now Nike designs its athletic styles at the same time, using the same technology for men's and women's styles and offering several color options for each.

When I walk into a Nike store today almost half of the sneaker wall is women's shoes and there are many colors to choose

---

102 (Gray 2018)

from. My biggest challenge when shopping for new sneakers is deciding which style to buy. This is a welcome change.

Nike has updated its approach to street sneakers as well. Up until recently, most styles were men's only, and most stores only carried a size 8 and higher. A men's size 8 translates to roughly a size 9.5 for women. Since the average woman's shoe size is between a size 8.5 and 9, the lack of smaller sizes limited the number of women that could even buy the men's version.

In 2015 at the Brooklyn Museum's "The Rise of Sneaker Culture" exhibit, Susan Boyle, owner of Brooklyn-based sneaker boutique Rime and the first non-designer woman to collaborate with Reebok, spoke on a panel with other professional women in the sneaker industry. During the panel, Susan spoke to the fact that women's sneakers are still largely an afterthought by most top brands.

"There is so much cool stuff for guys and it doesn't come in our size. Or if it does, they'll take something out and tweak it a little different, use cheaper material, or change the silhouette. They're not thinking about us, who we are, and I think that's one of the biggest problems we have," said Susan.[103]

---

103 (Bobila 2015)

Women love street sneakers too, and after years of voicing their frustration about limited options, brands like Nike are responding. Making its focus on women's products official, Nike launched the Unlaced initiative in early 2018. In it, Nike commits to offer smaller sizes of several popular men's sneaker styles, more color options in women's performance sneakers, and include the influence of more women through female-led collaborations with female designers.

For its 2018 Air Max Day, when new styles are released, Nike began offering its second women-only Air Max model, the Air Max Jewel (the first was the women's Air Max 1 shoes introduced in 1987). Another release was the women's version of the Air VaporMax. For the design, Nike collaborated with style consultant Aleali May who grew up in L.A., has been wearing fashionable sneakers since childhood, and has worked as a stylist and collaborator for other sportswear brands. A third change was the release of five Air Jordan 1s and five Air Force 1s that were designed by a group of 14 women, for women, and released in early 2018.[104]

While women's focused styles and color options are most certainly welcome, sometimes women don't necessarily want their own style, they want the same silhouette offered for men but in their size. That is why the decision

---

104 (Bobila 2018)

to offer smaller sizes of popular men's sneaker styles is such a big deal.

Highsnobiety senior staff writer Lia McGarrigle explained in a 2018 article saying, "Expanded sizing for major sneaker releases has been the best thing to happen to the industry in a long time — finally, sneakerheads with smaller feet aren't being left out."

Talking further about what all these changes mean for women, Lia went on to say, "More women-led sneaker campaigns and female sneaker designers are also really impactful. Instead of male executives deciding what we want, having women in charge doesn't only result in better sneakers, but it shows that the industry actually cares about our opinions."[105]

Efforts like these marks a shift in the importance of top brands like Nike recognizing there is still a lot more they can do to appeal to a broader range of women's preferences from athletic to street sneakers. Keep the changes coming.

**

As seen with street sneakers, sometimes women don't want a unique design, they just want the same product as men

---

105 (Bruzas 2018)

but sized appropriately. When it comes to athletic clothing there are several options that work across genders like joggers, track suits, hats, and sweatshirts.

For instance, a hoodie is just a hoodie no matter who's wearing it. Regardless of the logo on the tag, most hooded sweatshirts have a hood with draw cords and a front pocket. Sometimes adjusting a product's design for women is necessary and sometimes it's not. For instance, sometimes women want the hoodie design updated to be more feminine and other times they may want the same NFL team hoodie offered to men but in their size.

Many popular sneaker and casual shoe brands and styles already do this, including Converse, Van's, and Toms. The same shoe silhouette is worn by both men and women but offered in sizes for both genders.

ALLBIRDS

New brands like Allbirds have had a lot of success offering the same style to both men and women. Launched in 2016, Allbirds is a San Francisco-based shoe company offering environmentally friendly fashionable casual sneakers. Best known for their first style, Wool Runners, Allbirds is a certified B Corporation whose mission is to provide simply-designed, comfortable, eco-friendly footwear made with natural materials and sustainable manufacturing practices.

The founders, Tim Brown, a former professional New Zealand soccer play and Joey Zwillinger, an engineer from San Francisco, recognized the lack of fashion-forward casual shoes available on the market.

In an interview with CNBC, Brown stated, "In the middle of the footwear market, the casual footwear market, what I like to call the Foot Locker world, there was a bunch of what was seemingly average product which hadn't had a lot of innovation. Brands like Nike offered great performance footwear, but not many casual options."[106]

Along the lines of athleisure, what has made Allbirds so popular is that the shoes are *very* comfortable and have a fashionable minimalist design that is versatile enough to be worn to work but also for a workout. Their marketing focuses on the company's mission statement and product design.

Instead of designing one shoe for women and another for men, the brand launched with two styles offered to both men and women in the same colors but size options for each. Men

---

106 (Findling 2017)

and women are featured throughout the Allbird's site in the same way down to the way they are styled and posed. The only difference between the men's and women's sections on the site is the gender of the person wearing the shoes. Otherwise, the shoe colors, page layout, copy used on the page, and information provided is nearly identical.

In the first two years, Allbirds sold over a million pairs of Wool Runners, roughly $100 million in sales.[107] In September 2018, the brand opened its first store in New York City and has plans to open eight more throughout 2019.[108] Not bad for a startup that launched with two styles online.

How are women responding? In a 2018 interview with Yahoo, the founders noted that about 55 percent of their customers are female and 45 percent male. Their most popular color is grey.[109]

**

Using the color pink for women's products was never the issue. The issue was the assumptions around the color that justified the lack of other color options, attention, resources,

---

107 (Schneider-Levy and Abel 2018)
108 (Thomas 2018)
109 (Abel 2018)

and care provided to women's products…especially in the male dominated sports industry.

From "shrink it and pink it" to female-focused collaborations, campaigns, and product, brands in the sports industry have recognized that women are not an afterthought; they are half the population with significant buying power. As such, *women's products should be given the level of attention required to earn their purchases.*

Sometimes women want something different from men, and sometimes women simply want the same product offered to men. Smart brands will include women as part of the strategy and design process to figure out how best to approach apparel and footwear for women. Similarly, involving women in the marketing approach is also a winning strategy.

After dealing with limited options for years, women have responded overwhelmingly positive to having more and stylish options to choose from.

MEN SHOULD DESIGN WOMEN'S CLOTHES

---

f you weren't already aware, men have historically made most of the decisions around women's clothing, including design and style.

From the first couturier, Charles Fredrick Worth, who established the first haute couture house in Paris in 1858 and coined the term "fashion designer," to the designers of today, there is a long tradition of fashion being driven by male designers and leaders...who have never actually worn women's clothing...

Seeing and experiencing the design of clothes are not the same, whether a beautiful dress or sports apparel. There's a reason why the first thing so many women do when they come home from work is change into more comfortable clothes. Most women's clothing has been designed for looks, not life.

Take something as simple as pockets, for instance. Have you ever thought about why women carry purses? If you think about it, most women's clothing does not offer functional pockets. If pockets *are* sewn in, they are often too small to hold much of anything or are decorative faux pockets to allow for a form-fitting silhouette.

The absence of pockets in women's clothing is about more than the ability to carry a wallet, keys, and phone without the use of a purse. As Virginia Theerman, one of two writers on FIT's exhibit, "Pockets to Purses: Fashion + Function" told *Moneyish* in 2018, "There is definitely a sense of mobility and independence tied in with pockets; an ease of access, the ability to be on the move quickly instead of worrying, 'What if I forget (my purse) or lose it, or it's too full and I can't find anything in it?'"[110]

What would clothes look like if women were designing them and leading the companies making them? Well first, the clothes would have more pockets, but beyond that there's

---

110 (Pesce 2018)

really only one way to find out. More women need to be a part of the leadership and design for all women's clothing.

As we've already seen throughout this book, women have been pioneers for clothing at various times, from bloomers to the sports bra. Increasingly, more women are creating female-focused clothing designs that are attractive and practical. Market opportunity aside, all of these women are up against a strong headwind.

Across all business, women are largely excluded from senior roles. Among the Fortune 500 CEOs in 2018, there were almost as many men named John (23) as there were female CEOs (25).[111] Rather than working to support someone else's vision, some women decide to build their own path, which isn't exactly easier. In 2015, only 15 percent of all venture capital funding went to women, declining to 2 percent in 2017.

The activewear segment doesn't fare much differently, but women like Katie Johnson, co-founder of the women's activewear e-commerce destination Carbon38, are openly discussing the challenges female entrepreneurs face. In 2017, Katie told Emily Dunn in an interview with the *Huffington Post*, "Only 3 percent of all startups led by female CEO's

---

111   (Miller, Quealy, Sanger-Katz 2018)

secure funding. We *must* change that statistic. If we want balanced perspective in our board rooms, in our communities, and in our government, we need to cultivate diversity of thought."[112]

On a larger scale, according to the 2015 EY report, *Where will you find your next leader?*, only 4.8 percent of the CEOs of Fortune 500 companies in the U.S. are women. This percent is greater than worldwide, where women make up only 3.4 percent of CEOs.[113] Influence is not limited to female CEOs, but it is an interesting barometer for where women currently stand. There's much room for improvement across the board.

The discussion about the importance of women's participation in sports comes full circle because many of today's most powerful female leaders played sports growing up. Women's sports participation means a great deal more than maintaining a healthy lifestyle.

In speaking with several female founders and leaders in the athleisure space, I found that most of them were active growing up or became active in early adulthood. Initially, I thought that was an obvious connection since these women

---

112 (Dunn 2017a)
113 (EY and espnW 2015)

were part of the athletics industry. What I learned is the connection between sports and leadership is not limited to the athletic space.

To explore the connection between sports and women's professional lives, EY and espnW conducted a three-year research study released in 2015. The research found that sports is a powerful way to advance women in society. Gender parity in sports helps lead to greater gender parity in the boardroom.

Seventy-four percent of executive women said a sports background can help accelerate a woman's career, and 61 percent believe sports involvement has contributed to their own career success. However, this isn't just a belief. The study found that 94 percent of women in the C-suite played sports, 52 percent of which at a university level, and that many powerful women leaders have sport backgrounds.[114]

Despite the challenges they faced, several women not only started activewear or lifestyle brands, but also have been successful in growing them, collectively helping to expand the market for women's activewear. These female-led brands, often built by former athletes or fitness instructors, grow through female communities, and offer leadership roles for women.

---

114 Ibid

As Katie Johnson told me, "We work with 215 brands; most of which are female founded and led. That is rare in fashion, let alone in active where the big players are all male-founded and run, but that's true of all fashion. Eighty-five percent of womenswear brands are creatively directed, founded, and run by men."

Women supporting women who design fashionable activewear—I like the sound of that. I also like the sound of women creating leadership opportunities for themselves and other women that encourage the development of future leaders through athletics.

To further correct the gender imbalance and help female designed and led brands succeed, I believe it is important for women to support companies that support women. While men founded the top activewear companies of today, the top brands of tomorrow may have already been or will be founded and run by women in the future.

There are numerous athletic brands that women have started in recent years. I've chosen to highlight a few in the hopes of showing how these women are adding something different to the space and the challenges they've overcome to do that.

**

All women are athletes, but not all athletes exercise the same way, so there's a need for options around fit, style, and performance based on how each woman chooses to be active. Instead of waiting for another brand to provide what they were looking for, some women decided to build their own female led and female designed brands.

Some of these women were looking to create styles that focused on fashion over function while others created function over fashion. The result is that all women now have more options to work out in and wear as athleisure.

Many of these women grew their businesses through connecting with communities of women, whether through social media, fitness communities, or both. The communities that women have built are a place to share information, provide support, give feedback, and enable the growth of these new brands if they are able to connect with enough women.

Lorna Jane

Lorna Jane Clarkson is the founder of Lorna Jane and has been credited with coining the word "activewear" in 1989.[115] Women in the U.S. may not be as familiar with the brand

---

115 (Sherlock 2017)

because Lorna founded her brand in Brisbane, Australia in 1989. Her first U.S. store opened in California in 2012.

As of 2018, most of Lorna Jane's U.S. stores are located in California with stores throughout western states and Hawaii. Beyond the 250 stores across Australia and the U.S., Lorna Jane has stores in Europe, the UK, Africa, Asia, and the Middle East.

What's interesting to note about Lorna's story is she didn't set out to invent activewear or start a brand at all. The decision to create Lorna Jane happened rather organically. In the late 1980s Lorna worked as a dental therapist and part-time aerobics instructor. *Uninspired by the options available for women to wear to the gym, Lorna began designing and sewing her own designs.*

Lorna talked about how she got started in an interview with the online site The Cool Career, saying, "I never really planned to launch Lorna Jane as a fashion active brand. Being an aerobics instructor, I was constantly in activewear and back then, there was very little to choose from. So, one day I picked apart my favorite swimsuit, made a pattern and set about creating my own pieces in designs and colors I actually wanted to wear!"[116]

116 ("Lorna Jane Clarkson ⊠ Chief Creative Office + Founder / Lorna Jane Active Wear" 2018)

The women in her class would ask her about her clothes and if she could make pieces for them. After a few months, Lorna decided to commit herself to making activewear full-time and launched her own brand with her now husband Bill Clarkson in 1989.

Lorna and Bill opened their first store in Brisbane in 1990 and continued to open new stores every year, but getting started with concept stores, especially for activewear, was new. According to Lorna in a 2015 interview with The Australian, "Nobody believed in my concept...There was no focus on stylish activewear."[117]

But, Lorna wasn't one to back down from a challenge. "Back in the 1980s, I believed there was a retail category for activewear, but people who were not hard-core sports people thought I was crazy. The bottom line was if the concept didn't work, it didn't work," she said during the same interview.

Women were attracted to the technical but feminine designs of her line...so much so that the first week of sales was enough to cover the first month's rent, and in 1991 a customer purchased the entire store's stock for $25,000 to resell it. If that's not a sign a brand is on the right track, I don't know what is.

---

117 (Allen 2015)

Beyond the clothes, Lorna's vision is to promote an active life. As she is quoted on her activewear website, "if you wear activewear, you'll become more active." Lorna believes that leading an active life is just one aspect of overall wellness. While important for women to move their bodies every day, it's also important to nourish with food that provides nutrients and live with a positive mindset for long-term wellbeing.

The brand's motto "Move. Nourish. Believe." is represented by the brand's three icon logo. Still a private company, Lorna Jane has been estimated to be worth $500 million.[118]

OUTDOOR VOICES

Tyler Haney founded Outdoor Voices (OV) in 2013 with the mission to provide women with *technical apparel for recreation.* Tyler ran hurdles in high school and stayed active into college, deciding to study at Parson's School of Design in New York City.

Suited up in brightly colored running clothes while on a run one day, Tyler had the realization about the way she was dressed. Telling *Vogue* in 2018, "I just thought, Wait—I'm not

---

118 (The CEO Magazine 2018)

a track star!"[119] she said. Tyler recognized that most sports brands approached apparel as if women were training for competition, which gave her an idea. "What if I built a brand around something people loved—a *recreational* Nike that's all about staying healthy and being happy doing it?"

That's how Tyler sees OV as different. "With Nike and so many other brands, it's really about being an expert, being the best. With OV, it's about how you stay healthy—and happy."[120]

She became fascinated with technical fabric, searching for an option that performed but didn't look and feel like workout clothes. (You know, that shiny spandex that screams, *I am workout gear!*) Beyond the technical fabric, it was important to design pieces that were attractive. Instead of using neon colors that were popular for athletic clothes at the time, Tyler went in the other direction entirely, choosing to use earth and muted tone colors that were color blocked, and more recently adding polka dot to the mix.

However, at its core Outdoor Voices is focused on the function of its clothes because that will make or break a woman's experience and connect her to the brand, whereas design

---

119 (Sullivan 2018)
120 Ibid

trends come and go. As Tyler told *Outside Online* in 2018, "Fashion doesn't mean much for people anymore—experiences do, and activity is experience."[121]

While her mission was clear from the start, Tyler encountered a lot of resistance from potential investors who didn't understand what she was trying to build. Recalling her struggle, Tyler also told *Outside Online*, "I would go into a lot of guy investors' offices, and no one would get it," Haney says, recalling she was told "no" around 70 times. "But I started sending it to their wives ahead of the meetings, and that was really where the unlock came from."

Starting as an e-commerce brand, OV's community was built through social media and selling directly to customers. Most recently the brand created the hashtag #doingthings to encourage women to share how they are getting out and being active, or rather, *doing things*. Where other brands have built a following through athlete or celebrity collaborations, OV encourages women to create and influence their own active communities.

Starting out the brand leveraged the power of social media, influencers, and women's communities to establish itself. Through word of mouth and connecting with women

---

121 (Caplan-Bricker 2018)

directly, the brand grew a loyal following that helped it grow quickly.

Investors get it now. The results speak for themselves. Between 2013 and 2016, OV sales grew 800 percent,[122] and raised $34 million in a series C round in 2018, bringing total funding to almost $57 million.[123] At the end of 2018, OV had nine brick-and-mortar stores open with more coming soon.

CARBON38

Founded in 2013, Carbon38 was the first e-commerce destination that offered women the opportunity to shop a number of performance fashion brands in one place. Prior to launching Carbon38, Katie Warner Johnson, CEO & co-founder of Carbon38 studied at Harvard University, danced as a professional ballerina, and taught classes at Physique57, which allowed her to learn about the kind of activewear women liked and what flatters a woman's body.

Katie co-founded the company after she realized *there was an opportunity to provide the modern woman with versatile and flattering wardrobe options she can easily live her life in*. I was thrilled to have the chance to meet Katie, who

---

122 (Sullivan 2018)
123 (Thomas 2018)

spoke with passion about the industry, the Carbon38 customer, how she has grown her business, and the brands on
Carbon38.

"I think the change in demands on women's lives over the past
10 years is unprecedented. We have to enter the workforce
and win against all odds, raise the next wave of leaders, are
often the caretakers, have to maintain our relationships as
well as be kind and thoughtful," Katie told me.

Because of their demanding lifestyles women want beautiful
clothes that actually function. "As women, I think we have
risen to the occasion, but our wardrobes haven't. Where
I think there's an opportunity is active—it's easy to wear,
sexy, comfy, machine washable and as a result it's on trend.
It's what everyone wants to put on their body," Katie said.

She (and, in turn, Carbon38) also recognizes that women are
no longer limited to the trends that retailers dictate. Women
have options. "Now because you have your phone in your
hand and the entire internet to Google, you're choosing what
you want, when you want & you're not waiting for a stylist
or buyer to tell you," Katie said.

Performance is no longer enough. Women expect *all* activewear to perform. The difference between one brand and
another now lies in the design.

Understanding what women will respond to and finding those options is a priority for Carbon38. One of the ways they do so is through the fitness community, developing exclusive relationships in the fitness world by way of an ambassador fitness program with more than 3,000 fitness instructors.

Talking about the importance of understanding their customer Katie said, "We have a 360-degree view of our customer because we are tracking her—we are looking at what she buys, returns, and keeps. I've been obsessed with this customer for 10 years. I was her trainer and now I'm becoming her, so it's easy to have that conversation. I love hearing what she's wearing and what does and doesn't work."

Working with more than 200 brands, most of which are female founded and/or led, Katie and her team provide feedback, taking a hands-on approach because they "want to make sure everyone succeeds." Even when Carbon38 launched its own private label in 2015, they made it a point to be transparent about the designs with their 3rd party brands to avoid any surprises.

As of 2016, the company was outpacing sales of $20 million after growing over 500 percent the year before.[124] In 2018,

---

124 (Marikar 2016)

Carbon38 opened its first brick-and-mortar store in Los Angeles, California.

**

Beyond starting their own brands, it's also important for women to gain leadership positions within all companies. Even if women aren't the CEO or founder, including women in the design and decision-making process ensures a more female-focused outcome.

ATHLETA

Created to provide women with attractive and athletic workout clothes, Athleta has been female-centric from the beginning. Back in 2003, the company's founder Scott Kerslake told *The New York Times* that 95 percent of the 125 company employees were women. And, these women didn't just work for the company, some of them also wear-tested the clothes while training to make sure they performed well during a workout.[125]

Women also drove the design decisions, focusing on clothes that maintained a high level of performance for athleticism that was central to Athleta's brand. Quoted in the same *NYT*

---

125 (Warner 2013)

article, Ellen Krimmel, the design director at the time and a former professional cyclist said, "You have to be disciplined to say no to some products you know will sell, but aren't really Athleta."

Twenty years after the company was founded, the same female-led and female-focused tradition continues at Athleta with its current CEO Nancy Green and the added vision to empower all women to embrace their inner athlete.

In a 2017 interview with *The Huffington Post*, Nancy talked about the highlights of her role saying, "I get to make a difference, but more importantly WE get to make a difference – working with an amazing team, creating a product that meets a woman's unique needs; by breaking down stereotypes of female strength and beauty and uniting women to reach their limitless potential."[126]

Launched in 2016, the focus of the "Power of She" campaign embodies the brand's mission to create a "community of active, confident women and girls to reach their limitless potential and celebrates the power of sisterhood with the mantra 'Alone We Are Strong, United We Thrive.'" This includes *all* women, including employees who are often featured in Athleta marketing.

---

126 (Dunn 2017b)

"Athleta stands for inclusivity," Nancy Green stated in a press release speaking to the campaign message. "We want to break down stereotypes and help redefine perceptions of wellness and strength while celebrating the power of the female collective to make an impact."

In 2017, Nancy talked about the focus on women of all ages with *Racked* saying, "It's not only that young people want this, and old people want that, but we do understand that bodies do change as you get older, and the great things about the category that we're in is the fabrics that we use are unbelievable in terms of the performance, stretch, and comfort." Recognizing the commonality all women share Nancy said, "We know that what is most important to all of our customers, regardless of age, is versatility."[127]

Athleta uses a variety of real women of all ages in its catalog, creating a more authentic voice, focusing on helping women feel their best through comfortable and stylish clothes that also hold up for a workout. Equally as important, Athleta also recognizes the need to instill confidence among the next generation of women through sports.

"We found that 61% of female executives said athletic activities contributed to their success, so we see sports as

---

127 (Leiber 2017)

a multidimensional element to life," Sheila Shekar Pollak, Athleta's VP of Marketing, told *Marketing Dive* in 2018.[128]

This is relevant because as Sheila also noted, "By 14, girls' confidence plummets as 50% of girls drop out of sports — that's two times the rate that boys do. For girls who do stay in sports, their confidence levels dip less and go back up quicker. That really stopped us in our tracks, as both moms and athletes."

To help combat this challenge, Athleta launched the "Stay in the Game" campaign to encourage girls in elementary and middle school to continue playing sports and inspire them to lead active lives as they grow. Explaining the goal of the campaign further, Sheila said, "We aren't saying that all girls should be NCAA athletes or participate in the Olympics, but rather, that staying in sports helps to build confidence and friendships that can have a long-term impact on girls' daily lives."

Part of the campaign included videos depicting girls racing around a track, flipping tires and scoring during a soccer scrimmage while other two girls at microphones send a rally cry, proclaiming, "My sweat washes away self-doubt. I storm

---

128 (Koltun 2019)

the field unsure of all the things I'm capable of, but I know that quitting isn't one of them."

The more that young girls are told that strength and power are positive attributes for a woman to have, the more likely they are to stay in the game and be set up for success in the future. Sports empower.

**

It's not that men can't or shouldn't be behind the decisions concerning women's clothes, it's that women should be a much larger part of the conversation and creation beyond the role of a designer's muse.

As women's influence continues to increase because of key leadership positions in companies and industries that have been predominately male, how we approach and design for women will continue to become more authentic, female-focused, and impactful. We've already seen the positive impact that including female leaders in the conversation can have and expect this influence to grow over time.

Female led and female designed brands like Lorna Jane, Outdoor Voices, Carbon38, Athleta, and Sweaty Betty signal a shift in the right direction. Whether women are leading larger brands or starting their own, they are collectively making more of an impact in the sports apparel industry. Moreover, while some of these brands may be considered small compared to industry leaders, all it would take is for a few more to shift the dynamics further toward a female-designed and female-led industry.

But beyond apparel, there's a need to continue supporting the participation of girls and women in sports and fitness through access, encouragement, and of course, the right apparel to help them perform at their best. The connection between sports and success is undeniable, so it's important to set the next generation of women up for even greater achievement through sports opportunities.

What's that saying, "death by a thousand cuts?" Every purchase is a "vote." Female founders and leaders aren't the only ones responsible for driving change. Women that support female-led and focused brands and companies are contributing to the much-needed apparel evolution.

FALSEHOOD 10

ATHLEISURE IS
SUSTAINABLE

———

"Sustainability or responsible innovation is by far the biggest trend in the industry right now. And it's not a philanthropic quest – this is a business development," Eva Kruse, CEO of Global Fashion Agenda which organizes the Copenhagen Fashion Summit that brings together executives to talk about sustainability in the industry.[129]

At the current rate activewear sales are growing, in 2015 Morgan Stanley forecasted U.S. activewear sales to hit $83 billion in 2020.[130] Globally, in 2017 Morgan Stanley predicted

---

129 (Saner 2017)
130 ("Athletic Lifestyles Keep Apparel Sales Healthy" 2015)

sports apparel and footwear sales to hit $355 billion by 2021,[131] almost doubling from the $197 billion sales in 2007.

This is wonderful for women's comfort and style, and obviously, I'm a fan. On the other hand, most athleisure is made with synthetic fibers, which aren't exactly great for the Earth.

Remember when we all were in love with the touch, the feel of cotton, the fabric of our lives? Activewear and most athleisure clothing at this point is made with synthetic (i.e. man-made, not natural) fibers that are built to last a lot longer than you will. And, now that 49 percent of global fiber production is polyester, it has become the most used fiber in the apparel industry.[132]

While some brands have been focused on sustainable fabrics and practices for years, the increased manufacturing of synthetic fabric has brought the problem center stage. This is prompting other retailers, designers, and the launch of new brands to join efforts to provide innovative solutions.

Whether it's plastic water bottles or yoga pants, the same requests apply to reduce, reuse, and recycle.

---

131 ("Athletic Footwear Chases Fast Fashion" 2017)
132 ("Recycled Poly | Prana" 2018)

**

Athleisure is inherently built to last. Brands spend a lot of money innovating to create synthetic fabric that seemingly does it all – wicks away sweat and moisture, stretches to provide mobility, provides stability in areas that need it, and more. Except, while these properties are wonderful for a workout, the fabric isn't environmentally friendly. This is why being thoughtful with athleisure purchases is so important.

If you're asking yourself why synthetic fabrics are so bad, performance fabric is made with polyester fibers made from coal, air, water, and oil. This explains the moisture-wicking property of performance fabrics; oil and water don't mix. Simply put, polyester is made with a lot of chemicals.

Without getting too technical, some concerns that I have come across are that it requires twice as much energy to produce polyester than cotton, that microfibers from the synthetic fabrics shed during the washing process end up in our oceans, that synthetic fabrics have lower biodegradability, and the toxicity of the fabric can be transferred to the wearer.

These concerns have driven efforts to create more sustainable fabrics or increase the longevity of use to reduce the impact to the environment.

Driving these concerns are younger customers who prefer sustainable practices and products. Alice Goody, a retail analyst for Mintel, told *The Guardian* in 2017, "Forty-four percent of younger millennials – the 17-26 age range – said they would like to see more eco-friendly fabrics used in clothes."[133] Among other generations, 34 percent of Generation X and 30 percent of Baby Boomers noted eco-friendly fabrics were important to them.

Younger generations prefer brands and companies that have a mission larger than profit margin and will pay more for eco-friendly products that contribute to a sustainable lifestyle and humane labor practices. Therefore, instead of buying more, younger women are buying better. Mintel also noted that 69 percent of women surveyed between the ages of 25-44 are buying better items that can be worn longer rather than making more purchases. Fewer purchases mean less waste.

This shift in focus among younger customers will become more relevant as their buying power increases. Companies like Athleta recognize the importance of sustainable practices for the environment and customers.

Chris Samway, Athleta's Chief Financial Officer, talked with *B the Change* about the impact of the customer voice

---

133 (Hoguet 2017)

on their efforts saying, "From a purely financial perspective, the return on investment (ROI) associated with aligning interests of business with those of society is compelling. We know the next generation of consumers increasingly cares about brands that stand for something. We hear from our customers that putting people and planet right up there with profit is something that resonates with her."[134]

In 2018, Athleta made the commitment to become certified as a B Corporation with initiatives including the decision to use sustainable fibers in 80 percent of its fabrics, ensuring 25 percent of the products sold are made with water-saving techniques, and that 80 percent of waste from store packaging be diverted from a landfill by 2020.

What are B Corporations? According to the B Corporation website, they are "businesses that meet the highest standards of verified social and environmental performance, public transparency, and legal accountability to balance profit and purpose. B Corps are accelerating a global culture shift to redefine success in business and build a more inclusive and sustainable economy."

Patagonia, Allbirds, and The North Face are also B Corps, among others, so adding another player in the athletic

---

134 ("Create Employee Champions and Customer Advocates Around Your Mission" 2018)

apparel space like Athleta furthers the discussion around sustainable practices and shows how the customer voice is initiating change.

**

Quality clothing lasts, so in my opinion an initial investment to purchase well-made athleisure is worth it. Also, fewer purchases means less waste on the environment. I have activewear that I bought *years* ago and it still performs every week the way I need it to without looking worse for wear. Because of that, here's my secret...I rotate through the same activewear every week which means I don't actually purchase new gym clothes that often.

When it comes to my gym clothes, sneakers, and athleisure, I buy for longevity. This means that I usually purchase options that are on the pricier side with a relatively classic look because I know I'll be wearing them for *years* so I better like them! P.S. – I also make sure to take care of the clothes by properly washing and hang drying them to help them last even longer.

Anything I purchase that I don't end up wearing ends up donated or resold. I only throw away clothes that I would be embarrassed to donate and cannot resell, which means the fabric is worn past repair or the clothes have begun to smell like a gym.

Is spending around $80 or more a lot to spend on a pair of leggings? Yes, absolutely...especially if you don't plan to wear them often. *However,* will I wear those leggings over a hundred times? Probably. That's less than a dollar per wear depending on how long I keep them. Which, when you break it down, is actually quite affordable in the long term. Plus, if you purchase a style you love, there won't be any hesitation about wearing it over and over and over.

And not all of my leggings are expensive. With the number of brands offering athletic clothing now it's easy to find options that offer good quality at various price ranges. The key for me is to find the right combination of style and performance for whatever activity I'll be doing.

Now that I've built up quite a collection of more casual athletic clothing options, I find myself following the same pattern, questioning myself as to whether I *really* need that new shiny piece of athleisure and how often I'm really going to wear it. Let's be honest here, my heart *always* says yes, but my head and full closet usually say no. Sometimes my heart wins and I buy the unnecessary but at the time what feels so necessary jacket, top, or jogger. If I don't end up wearing it within a short time the item is usually returned, re-sold or donated.

**

Between 2000 and 2014, all clothing production doubled in response to lower costs, streamlined operations, and increased customer spending, causing the average number of clothes a consumer purchases each year to increase by 60 percent.[135] Much of this has more to do with the rise of fast fashion than activewear, but as athleisure has become more fashionable with options that are stylish and lower in price, similar to fast fashion, the lanes are merging. Many brands are coming out with new styles monthly to inspire more purchases.

The result of fast fashion is not only more purchases, but also more waste. Across all apparel, consumers are keeping their clothes about half as long as they did 15 years ago as lower priced items are viewed as disposable, often being discarded after being worn only seven or eight times.[136]

The longer clothes are used, the less waste is created, so re-use programs or donations help keep clothes in play longer. There

---

135 (Remy, Speelman, and Swartz 2018)
136 Ibid

are many alternatives to throwing away clothes. Almost 100 percent of textiles and clothing are recyclable so there really isn't a reason to throw any of them away.

If you're looking to get back money spent on clothes that can no longer be returned or are gently used, there are second hand resale options like Poshmark, ThreadUp, Facebook Marketplace, and eBay where clothes can be listed and re-sold. For each, all a seller has to do is set up an account, take a picture of the clothes, and upload them to the community.

As a seller, you may not get back much, depending on what you're selling, but something is better than nothing, right? In addition, as a buyer these online locations are great options if you want to try out a new brand or style without paying full price. For new athletes or someone getting into fitness for the first time, this provides a great way to start your new lifestyle in style without breaking the bank.

Alternatively, if selling online seems like too much of a hassle, there are other more straightforward options. Several retailers offer repairs or recycle programs to help keep more clothes out of the landfill, including Patagonia, Nike, and adidas.

**

One of the most conscious sports apparel brands invested in reducing the environmental impact of clothes is Patagonia, which was founded in 1973 by Yvon Chouinard as a rock-climbing store that sold rugby shirts and corduroy shorts. Today, it's known for outdoor gear.

Patagonia offers high quality performance gear in simple stylish designs that can be worn for activity or casual use for years because of their timeless look. Committed to sustainable practices, Patagonia works to reduce the environmental and labor impact of manufacturing as well as uses organic and recycled fabrics in over half of their clothes.

Beyond the company's actions, Patagonia also encourages customers to make sustainable purchase decisions by keeping their Patagonia garments in good condition and use for as long as possible. Focusing on reduce, repair, reuse, and recycle, Patagonia aims to limit the number of clothes recycled by increasing the lifetime use of the clothes already made, even if that means customers making fewer purchases.

As Rose Marcario, the current Patagonia CEO states on the brand's Worn Wear online site, "As individual consumers, the single best thing we can do for the planet is to keep our stuff in use longer. This simple act of extending the life of our garments through proper care and repair reduces the need to buy more over time—thereby avoiding the CO_2 emissions, waste output, and water usage required to build it."

Reduce discourages unnecessary purchases by providing customers with durable clothes that last. To extend the life of their clothes, Patagonia encourages customers to *repair* clothes that are still wearable instead of discarding them by offering a repair service that only charges a fair price for repairs that are a result of normal wear and tear.

To encourage more *reuse* of Patagonia clothes, the company offers the option for customers to trade in Patagonia gear in exchange for a credit that can be used to purchase a new or used garment. Items suitable for continued wear are resold on its Worn Wear online store. Items that cannot be resold are *recycled* into new fibers and fabric.

**

More than Patagonia, other brands are making efforts to increase their use of recycled materials, including Nike and adidas, without sacrificing how the clothes perform.

Product innovation isn't limited to performance at Nike. Nike's sustainability goals focus on three key areas – minimize environmental footprint, transform manufacturing, and unleash human potential – with many initiatives focused on 2020. As their 2017 annual report states, "At Nike, we exist to serve athletes. This pushes us to deliver performance, products, and services for athletes with zero compromise."

As of 2018, 75 percent of all Nike shoes and apparel contains some recycled material making them the largest user of recycled polyester. For instance, the VaporMax Air sole contains more than 75 percent recycled material. The brand's most eco-friendly shoes are made with Flyknit technology that stitches the entire upper sole of the shoe with one yarn, maximizing athletic performance while producing 60 percent less waste than traditional cut-and-sew methods.[137]

In addition to Nike, adidas and its collaborators are also doing what they can to use recycled materials in their clothes and commit to sustainable manufacturing practices.

Stella McCartney, whether partnering with adidas or designing her own line, has been a long-time eco warrior, including her partnership with adidas. In 2016, the Stella McCartney and adidas line launched a collection that was 38 percent sustainable, and in 2018 was able to introduce 100 percent recycled leggings.[138]

---

137 (NIKE, Inc. 2018)
138 (Farra 2018)

Talking to Refinery29 in 2016 about sustainability Stella said, "We're always considering the environment. That's important to us. It's important that when you buy and invest in a Stella McCartney and adidas piece that you know it's gonna be with you, hopefully, for life. We make the quality of what we do. It's not throwaway sportswear, and there's a lot of that out there now that can become landfill."[139]

Beyond its collaboration with Stella, key initiatives adidas has announced include cutting the amount of water its apparel material suppliers use in half, phasing out the use of virgin plastic from all its products, stores, and offices around the globe by 2020, cutting its waste in half, and trimming its key suppliers' energy consumption by 20 percent.

In 2017, adidas made headlines after it introduced three new versions of its popular UltraBoost shoe that were made out of plastic found in the ocean in partnership with the environmental initiative Parley for the Oceans. Each shoe was made from 11 recycled plastic bottles and over one million pairs were sold in 2017[140]...that's a lot of recycled bottles!

**

139 (Cunningham 2016)
140 (Nicholson 2018)

With the increased awareness and focus on the environmental impact of synthetic clothes, there has been an increase in the number of new brands offering more sustainable activewear options. One of those brands is Girlfriend Collective, which not only focuses on performance and sustainability but also inclusivity.

Girlfriend Collective speaks to the very nature of transparency and sustainability. Launched in 2016 by the husband-and-wife duo Quang and Ellie Dinh, the brand was launched to create a sustainable activewear brand for people who care – care about other people, care about how their clothes are made, and care about making an impact through their purchasing power. Quang told me they wanted to "be the change we wanted to see in the marketplace."

Their hope is to help people lead more sustainable lives and rethink the activewear industry's role in saving the earth. Each pair of leggings is made with 25 recycled water bottles in a fair trade facility that has been certified as safe. Even the dye process they use is eco-friendly; ensuring water used to dye their fabric is treated and cleaned before being returned to nature. Part of their mission includes transparency, so like the larger brands, the company offers information about its factories, dye processes, and labor practices on its website.

But, just because the clothes are sustainable doesn't mean quality is compromised. The technical fabric Girlfriend Collective uses was developed over the course of a year and road tested with over 100 women, gathering their likes and dislikes. Their Core Fabric offers compression for medium to high-impact workouts and post-workout recovery. Even the colors they use are inspired by nature like Apricot, Moss, and Plum–attractive colors that can be worn year after year.

Beyond sustainable, the brand is also inclusive. They offer high-waisted leggings in sizes XXS–6XL that are photographed on a diverse set of women across various sizes, ages, body types, and ethnicities. Bonus! The images are not retouched. It's like shopping in a dressing room with your girlfriends...

When I asked Quang why Girlfriend Collective decided to offer a broad size range, he responded, "It was a no brainer for us to make as many sizes as we could to outfit that base [who care], and we're constantly trying to make our line more inclusive. We offer sizes to that go up to 6XL in our leggings so more people can feel and look great working out."

Last, the leggings are offered at a price below industry leaders, making them affordable for women who are also budget-conscious.

Discussing the obstacles faced when the brand first launched, Quang said, "I think a lot of people thought that we were too good to be true and a scam, since we came out of nowhere with our campaign and this product. But once customers started wearing and trying out our leggings that customer skepticism eventually went away."

Mara Leighton described her experience wearing Girlfriend Collective leggings on *Business Insider*. She purchased and now owns almost 20 pairs of leggings that she wore regularly a couple of years ago when she was running almost 20 miles a week. The Girlfriend Collective leggings became her favorite and have yet to be unseated.

Describing why they are her favorite, Mara stated, "They're still dark black (even after many washes), the aforementioned seams follow the natural line of your body and slim as well as elongate legs, and the material and fit is still somewhat architectural, like a comfortable and slightly looser pair of Spanx. The no-pill material is slightly chicer than a normal athletic legging, so something about them feels "dressier" than my Lululemons, for example, which makes them easier to throw on for brunch or hanging out with friends."[141]

**

---

141 (Leighton 2018)

Despite all of these great initiatives there is still more to do, not just in terms of reducing waste, but improving the synthetic fabrics themselves. In addition to reduce, reuse, and recycle, we now need to *restrict* the impact of our decisions.

In 2018, awareness was raised about the impact that plastic straws have on the environment with several restaurants and locations restricting or banning the use of straws seemingly overnight. But, straws and other plastic you can see floating in the ocean it isn't the only plastic that ends up in it. Microplastic pollution, or tiny micro fibers that also find their way to the ocean, are a rising concern as well.

A 2017 International Union for Conservation of Nature and Natural Resources study found that microplastics contribute between 15 to 31 percent of marine plastic pollution versus large plastic items. Of all the sources for microplastics, which include laundered synthetic textiles, tire abrasion, city dust, personal care products, and plastic pellets, washing synthetic clothes contributes 35 percent of the total microplastic pollution.[142]

What does all of that mean? Well, every time we wash clothes made with synthetic fabrics, like activewear and athleisure, tiny fiber pieces break off and end up in the

---

142 (Boucher and Friot 2017)

ocean. This happens because currently, no water-treatment plants can catch all of the pieces. To make matters worse, the older the garment, the more fibers are shed during the washing process.

This means that customers like me who thought they were doing the right thing by wearing their synthetic clothes longer to reduce waste may actually be the worst offenders when it comes to microplastic shedding and pollution, regardless of the type of synthetic fabric or whether it's been recycled or not.

Once these fibers reach a local river or the ocean, "they act like sponges, sucking up other pollutants around them," explains the Story of Stuff project,[143] created to raise awareness and help to find solutions to this pollution. The fibers essentially become "little toxic bombs full of motor oil, pesticides, and industrial chemicals that end up in the bellies of fish and eventually in the bellies of us," the project goes on to describe. It's not an appetizing thought.

While brands and manufacturers continue to improve the sustainability of polyester and recycled polyester there are efforts consumers can make as well. One is to wash your clothes less frequently. I'm not suggesting to re-wear your

---

143 (The Story of Stuff Project 2018)

clothes after an intense run, but if you wear a fleece out casually on the weekend, you could probably put it back in your closet for another use instead of in the washing machine at the end of the day.

To reduce the impact of micro shedding while laundering your athleisure, wash in cold water and use liquid detergent instead of powder. There are also fiber-collective devices available that can be put into the washing machine to catch the micro-fibers during the wash cycle. A couple of options include placing clothes a bag to trap the fibers or adding a ball to the wash cycle that rolls around and catches the fibers. Every little bit helps, right?

Ideally, new materials that do not shed at all can be developed as well as improvements to washing machines and waste treatment plants to capture stray fibers. These improvements will take time, money, and resources. And, while brands like Patagonia are researching solutions, we need more manufacturers, apparel companies and customers to be aware and to be active participants in the solution.

**

The benefits of performance fabric should not be at the cost of our planet and fellow humans. The technical nature of synthetic fabric used for athletic clothes means they provide benefits that natural fibers don't, which is great for athletes and those of us who enjoy the comfort of athleisure, but there are downsides.

While sustainable initiatives have been in place with some brands for years, all brands and customers need to be aware and involved to reduce environmental impact. The increase in purchases of synthetic fabric clothing has intensified the focus and actions to find ways to produce quality products with minimal impact to the environment.

Also, it's not just about athleisure. There's a need for all apparel and footwear brands to evaluate what they can do to reduce pollution throughout their supply chain. Beyond those already mentioned, other brands, designers, and companies focused on sustainability initiatives include Eileen Fisher, Levi's, Alternative Apparel, Everlane, Armour Vert, and H&M.

While younger customers may be the most vocal about their desire for sustainable practices, products, and brands, all of us have a responsibility to put our dollars where our hearts are and support programs, businesses, and brands that are actively making strides to eliminate the impact to our environment. Beyond this, it's up to consumers of these products to make good purchasing and care decisions to maximize the use of clothes made with synthetic fabric and minimize their impact on the environment.

Whether all of us or none of us decides to reduce, reuse, and recycle clothes, everyone will be impacted.

ATHLEISURE HAS LIMITED INFLUENCE

The impact of athleisure isn't limited to the rise in sales of yoga pants and sportswear. That would be too easy. Now that more women have seen what it is to be comfortable and stylish, there's a desire for more of their wardrobe to inherit many of the same characteristics as athletic clothing.

Yes, athleisure, athletic clothing, streetwear, sportswear... whatever you want to call it...will continue to influence each other and grow in popularity over the next several years. However, beyond these clothes there are impacts to other types of apparel women wear. Stretch, comfort, and performance are becoming a larger part of women's apparel, regardless of whether the clothes are sports related.

Fueling this change is that women are pushing back on the expectations of what they should wear, choosing clothes and brands that speak to real women rather than market an ideal. Women want clothes that fit them where they are, not where they "should" be based on cultural definitions of beauty and size. As a result, women are responding to brands with an authentic message and options that fit them and their lifestyle. Brands that don't evolve will struggle to maintain relevance.

Women's desire for changes to their clothing is evident across their wardrobe. Jeans are being updated to include more stretch, lingerie has become more size inclusive, and performance fabric used in activewear is being designed as part of everyday work wear.

And, even if women's love of athleisure wanes in the next few years the impact of women's desire for comfort, inclusion, style, and versatility are only going to evolve, not reverse. The new game is already in motion, so there are two options—learn the rules to win or sit the game out and hope for the best. I'd personally recommend the former option.

JEANS BECAME STRETCHY

What we have learned from the rise in popularity of leggings is that women like stretchy pants. They don't like it when pant waist bands dig into them or the fit is uncomfortable. Women continue to style their outfits with the same care, but with leggings instead of jeans. The result—leggings sales increased, denim sales decreased.

Jeans had been *the* pant of choice for casual occasions for years, but that has slowly changed as leggings have grown in popularity. Now women have an alternative. One of the women who transitioned from jeans to leggings is Erin Mayo, who lived in Texas when she swapped her jeans for leggings after seeing how comfortable other women looked in them.

"When I had a job where I wore scrubs every day, I used to spend money on cute weekend clothes and would attend activities like a birthday party or school events in them," Erin told me. "After a while I realized that the other women were dressed in some version of athletic wear – whether casual or expensive looking. I asked myself, 'why am I wearing jeans when no one else is?' I felt uncomfortable and stiff when everyone else looked cute and more comfortable."

Now, Erin is styling her athleisure outfits with the same enthusiasm she put into her weekend wardrobe. "When I go to my daughter's parties and activities now, I'm wearing the same type of clothes as the other women. Now that I'm in it, I've been sucked down the rabbit hole."

Talking about how she styles her outfits, Erin told me, "You *can* make athleisure cute and have fun with it. I wear the pieces differently than the other women do but that's the fun of it. You can express your own personality. There's also so many ways you can wear it—it's very versatile—you can wear it at the gym, on the weekend, or incorporate it into outfits during the week."

If you've read this far into the book you know that Erin is not alone in her desire for comfort and decision to wear and style athletic clothing for leisure use. A study by Synchrony Financial in 2016 found that 69 percent of those surveyed said they wear athleisure clothing, as opposed to jeans, at least once a week, especially among younger customers.[144]

Marc Cohen, director of retail studies at Columbia Business School acknowledged the shift telling *The Washington Post* in 2017, "All you have to do is look around. Ten years ago, it was cool to be wearing a pair of very expensive designer jeans, but now it's very much not cool. All the fashionable women are wearing yoga pants."[145]

In the early 2000s premium denim jeans rose in popularity, commanding as much as $350 or more for a pair. For

---

144 ("5 Retail Trends to Watch" 2016)
145 (Bhattarai 2017)

example, between 2007 and 2012, business tripled for the ever-popular premium denim brand True Religion. Such gains changed direction soon afterward as sales dropped 25 percent from 2013 to 2016, while women's activewear sales increased. As of 2017, the U.S. Census Bureau reported that elastic knit pants (i.e. leggings and yoga pants) imports exceeded those of jeans for the first time.[146]

Compared to the $350 price tag of premium denim jeans, a pair of $98 leggings from Lululemon looks like a bargain, and once women became accustomed to the comfort of leggings, they started to look for the same from their jeans. Brands like Levi's responded by adding more stretch to their styles.

Obviously, the slowdown in sales was noticed by the denim industry. In a July 2015 interview with Bloomberg, Levi's CEO Chip Bergh responded to the rise in athleisure clothing sales and decline in jeans sales. "We're scrambling. I mean, there is a big difference between the product that we've got on the floor today and what the consumer is looking for. And we just flat-out missed it," he said.[147]

146 (Bhasin 2018)
147 ("Denim's Demise: How Athletic Wear Is Impacting the Jean Business" 2016)

To say that jeans are not a forgiving piece of clothing is an understatement in my experience. I know I'm not the only woman to quickly say a prayer before attempting to put on a pair of jeans and then spending the next few minutes jumping up and down and squatting to get them on properly, *especially* after being washed. It's not difficult to see how stretchy pants such as yoga pants would become a preferred option to wear.

In 2016, Levi's updated classic styles. In a press release the company explained, "For the first time in its 143-year history the 501® and 501® CT jeans are getting the stretch treatment."[148] Spending a year to get the fabric right, Levi's made sure that the stretch was incorporated into the feel but maintained the same classic look the 501®'s were known for.

Levi's chief marketing officer Jen Sey told Business of Fashion in2017, "Stretch is here to stay," noting the company saw an increase in demand for stretch denim.[149] Beyond Levi's, other brands not only added stretch to their jeans but now market it as a selling point.

As much as leggings have become another staple of women's wardrobes, denim has remained so. "She might wear [leggings]

---

148 ("Levi's® Iconic 501® Jeans Gets the Stretch Treatment" 2016)
149 (O'Connor 2017)

to brunch with her friends on a Sunday, but she wasn't going to wear them out on a date on a Saturday night, and she wasn't going to wear them to work," Jen also said. "Denim has a foothold in certain occasions that leggings never will."

While there are women who do wear leggings to work and for date night, Jen has a point in that many of the women I spoke with echoed the sentiment that leggings are still not appropriate for all occasions, *for now at least*. Jeans are considered the dressy casual option that women wear then they do not believe that wearing athleisure is acceptable for the event they are attending.

Even still women, including me, want jeans to be more comfortable. Now, thanks to women's demand for comfort there are more comfortable jeans with stretch available.

TECHNICAL FABRIC EXTENDS INTO MORE APPAREL

Why should fabric used for activewear be limited to sports? As we've seen with sportswear, streetwear, and now athleisure, there is an appetite for fabric that is more often used for athletes to also be used in everyday clothes.

If you've ever lived in a city and walked to work or taken public trains in July like I have, you may also understand how moisture-wicking has a place in work clothing. More than moisture-wicking and comfort, the elimination of dry cleaning and ironing are two additional reasons why I'm a fan of performance fabric than more technical business casual clothing. Imagine if your work clothes were as easy to take care of as your gym clothes. Wouldn't that be a dream?

It seems as though that dream may become a reality. "We're starting to see more and more performance fabrics entering into what I would call classic apparel," Matt Powell, VP and Senior Industry Advisor for The NPD Group, Inc. told Yahoo Finance in 2017.[150]

Among others, Athleta has already ventured into this space, offering clothes made from technical fabric with the same performance characteristics as athletic clothing like moisture-wicking, stretchy, breathable, quick-drying but for primarily street use. For example, Athleta offers a whole line of "City Pants" that are made for active and casual endeavors, like travel or a day of walking as well as button down shirts made with performance fabric and other options.

I'm personally a huge fan of these clothes because they look more like what some refer to as "real clothes" but they feel as comfortable as athleisure and bonus, are easier to care for.

---

150 (Roberts 2017)

Whether I'm wearing one of the button-downs made from technical fabric or pants, the outfits I can put together look like a relaxed and sporty version of business casual.

Since these clothes are not intended to be used for sports, they could be considered traditional sportswear like casual button-down shirts that have a sporty look. However, the use of technical fabric still differentiates them into a grey area between sportswear and athleisure.

Because it seems everything must have a name these days, a new term has been created to describe comfortable, stylish, and versatile office-appropriate clothing made from technical fabric. These clothes have been referred to as *workleisure,* a derivative of athleisure, naturally.

New brands are also emerging that are speaking squarely to this type of clothing—classic casual and even business clothes made with performance and technical fabrics. Not limiting the use of performance fabric to athletic apparel, these brands are taking the benefits of technical fabrics beyond the gym to the office and streets.

One of those new brands is ADAY. Launched in 2015 by Nina Faulhaber and Meg He, ADAY focuses on casual simple designs made with intelligent technical fabrics for travel, work, exercise, and life in general. The brand's mission is to create a wardrobe that does more with less by offering classic silhouettes with a modern design that the women can wear season after season.

Essentially, ADAY offers updated casual clothing with performance fabric. Or, as Nina told me, ADAY is "reimagining wardrobe staples but with better fabrics." Also founded with sustainability in mind, many of the garments use recycled materials and/or are manufactured in factories that use solar and biomass energy to produce.

ADAY offers a range of options from their most popular Something Borrowed Shirt (a button down) and their Back to Front Shirt (a button down shirt dress that can be worn front-to-back or back-to-front) to various leggings and track pants that can be worn casually, traveling, or for exercise.

Launching with just seven pieces, the brand has expanded to offer 30 with the goal to grow intentionally, only adding styles they intend to offer forever. And to help women get more use out of each piece, ADAY shows women different ways they can style each piece for their active lifestyle. The thought is that if women buy pieces that are versatile and can be worn several ways, there will be less of a need to buy more.

Describing her passion for sustainability and minimalism, Nina told me, "From a macro standpoint, if you're in a business of creating things, which we are – a product, brand, community etc. – you're ultimately defining what the future should look like in your small way and contribution. We have such a big responsibility to make sure that the future we are creating is the best, most beautiful future possible."

Going on to discuss how that translates into ADAY's designs, Nina said, "I think with the minimalist aesthetic there is an opportunity to build a wardrobe of the future our customers and we love. We want our customers to wear these pieces every single day. We want the clothes to be beautiful, comfortable, and versatile, but also have benefits that help planet earth to last longer and have a better future," she said.

To get the design right ADAY listens closely to customer feedback through their site, surveying customers and using testing groups. In fact, Nina told me that over 7,000 women have applied to be wear-testers for the brand through their site application! The testing program, like all other feedback, is used to improve their designs.

In 2018, ADAY was named one of the World's Most Innovative Companies by Fast Company and had raised over $2 million in venture capital funding, including from H&M Co:Lab, H&M's venture capital fund.

And beyond technical fabric, there are several other new or established brands that have launched over the past several years that are focused on providing women with elevated casual clothes that are suitable for the street or even work including Modern Citizen, Lou & Grey, and Everlane.

The middle ground of modern clothing options for women that sit between accessible, sporty, and comfortable will continue to grow over the next several years as women begin to redesign clothes for work and play that are accessible, versatile, and fit with the modern woman's lifestyle.

LINGERIE IS REDEFINED

Like the sports bra, women want their regular undergarments to fit comfortably. Part of the athleisure trend has included wearing stylish sports bras that have built-in cups as well as interesting back strap designs that are stylish enough to be worn on their own or seen peeking through a loose-fitting exercise top. I wouldn't say these bra options provide a lot of support for a workout but they are comfortable for casual or low impact exercise.

Nevertheless, these stylish sports bras have inspired more of an athletic take on lingerie. Similar to the stylish sports bras, bralettes, which are bra-like in shape but are essentially a piece of fabric without the structured cups and push-up features many bras provide, have become popular among younger women.

Most notably, these sportier bras create a more natural look, which is different from the popular sculpted fantasy look women have worn in recent years. You know, when half of your chest disappears after you remove your bra.

For years, brands like Victoria's Secret (VS) have been a staple in most women's dresser drawers with their push-up bras and sexy messaging, but that seems to be changing. Brands focusing on inclusivity and comfort are resonating with women more these days. Instead of going for what's considered sexy, women are choosing options that are comfortable and have a more natural fit.

Over the past two years, Google Trends, a website that shows the popularity of search queries in Google Search, shows that searches for "bralette" surged over the "push-up bra" in 2015, maintaining a lead of two to three times as many searches for bralette as push-up bra in the United States into 2018. And, almost predictably at this point, the market research company NPD Group reports that the highest priority among millennial women in regard to their bras is "comfort".[151]

---

151 (The NPD Group, Inc. 2016)

"The comfort and wearability of the athleisure apparel trend, that is embedded in the Millennial style vocabulary, will compel them to seek the same type of comfort and ease of movement throughout their bra journey; this ultimately drives them toward different shopping behaviors than those of Boomers and older generations," noted Marshal Cohen, chief industry analyst of The NPD Group, Inc. in reference to a 2015 Bra Journey Insights report.

More than search terms and analyst reports, 2018 saw Victoria's Secret struggle to maintain customer interest in its ever popular semi-annual sale. As long as I can remember, the Victoria's Secret semi-annual sale was a big deal. In fact, I would purposefully steer clear of the store during the event while at the mall because it was usually mobbed with women. Not exactly the most financially savvy move, but the best one for my sanity for sure.

Fast-forward to 2018 and things have changed a bit. In June 2018, the same month as its famous semi-annual sale, Victoria's Secret saw a one percent same store sales decline. In fact, there were so few customers coming into the store to shop the sale that the company extended the sale two more weeks and reduced prices even further. Even still, the sale that used to drive sales up wasn't able to deliver like it had in years past.

This decrease in customers and sales is not recent. The company had been struggling throughout the year with its stock falling more than 45 percent in 2018. "We believe this all means the brand is broken," noted Jefferies financial analyst Randal Konik to CNBC.[152]

The likely culprit has to do with again, a change in women's preferences. Serena Rees, who cofounded Agent Provocateur, a sexy lingerie brand in 1994 told *The Guardian* in 2018, "Brands such as Victoria's Secret, La Perla, and even Agent Provocateur have become over-sexualized, and it's not relevant to this generation anymore."

Speaking to the changes in women's preferences more specifically Serena said, "What I did in the '90s was socially and politically for that moment. Now, we don't want to be dressed up in stockings and suspenders; we don't want to parade around for anybody. We're about comfort: streetwear, sportswear."[153]

I couldn't have said it better myself.

Conversely, brands like American Eagle's Aerie are seeing success with a different and more inclusive approach.

---

152 (Brassil 2018)
153 (Harper 2018)

Launching a new campaign in 2018, "Aerie Bras Make You Feel Real Good," the Aerie brand is challenging the current market leader with bras that are pretty but comfortable and embrace a women's desire for authenticity. Yes, they still sell push-up bras, but they also sell several other non-padded options with and without wires, and of course, bralettes.

Instead of showing airbrushed images and supermodels, Aerie shows its bras and underwear on real women of all shapes, sizes, ages, and ethnicities, including two-time Olympic gymnast Aly Raisman. Best of all, the women modeling the lingerie have not been Photoshopped to perfection, reflecting more accurately what a real average woman will look like wearing their products…a stark contrast to the Victoria's Secret branding.

Choosing to show women's bodies as they are makes a statement. After years of looking at clothes and lingerie on pictures of women who have been airbrushed and strategically posed, some may refer to the realities of stretch marks and cellulite as body imperfections. I call them being a woman. Plus, I find it's a lot more enjoyable to shop for clothes that are modeled on women who look more like I do.

How are customers responding? With purchases. Aerie has had 15 financial quarters of same-stores sales growth, or almost four years of growth. And, according to the company, younger shoppers *and* their moms are buying.[154]

**

Adding it all up, the impact of athleisure demonstrates a complete shift toward a new way of dressing that is comfortable, authentic, and makes life a little easier, and just because women are moving in this direction doesn't mean they are giving up their desire for stylish outfits.

Instead, women create their outfits by choosing or adding different pieces, and in doing so redefine what constitutes appropriate clothing across all occasions. There's something to be said about strength in numbers. When enough women follow the same path it becomes clear what women are looking for and the direction they are choosing to go.

Throughout this chapter and various points in this book it's clear that younger generations of women, be it Millennials or Gen Z, are driving many of the shifts in clothes. Unlike previous generations that had different clothes for each occasion, younger women are finding ways to merge elements of their casual clothes with their formal clothes. Why choose when you can have both?

---

154 (Howland 2018)

And more than clothes, women are communicating with the brands they support and the products they buy that the message a brand sends is as important as the clothes they offer. The brand and its messaging go hand in hand, so when the product isn't right, it's likely the messaging has missed the mark as well.

Whether finding creative ways to incorporate athleisure into their outfits or demanding the clothes be updated to fit their needs better, there's a clear pattern that today's fashion is influenced by athleisure and what women love about it. Yoga pants didn't just initiate the athleisure trend, they started a ripple effect that grew into a full-fledged fashion movement that doesn't show signs of slowing down.

FALSEHOOD SUMMARIES & CONCLUSION

If you've read this far you know the title of each chapter is *obviously* a falsehood. So, let's recap all of the "falsehoods" and talk about what that means for athleisure in the future.

**

Athleisure is a trend is a falsehood because a trend is time bound in that it rises in popularity and then declines over time. Athleisure continues to climb and sustain its popularity with women because it represents more than merely a fashion trend; it's a shift in mindset around the way women want to dress and live their lives. From women beginning to wear pants in the early 1900s to suits in the 1920s, athleisure is the latest advancement in women's decision to dress how they *want* instead of how they *should* dress.

**

Athleisure started as fashion is a falsehood because athleisure is rooted in sports. By definition athleisure is athletic clothing worn for leisure, so you need the "ath" to get athleisure. But before the "ath" could come, women had to earn the right to participate in sports and be treated as the legitimate athletes they are.

Through the passing of Title IX, women's sports participation and resulting need for athletic clothes to wear grew exponentially. Unlocking women's participation in sports was a turning point for many aspects of women's lives. Women became stronger, both physically and mentally through physical activity, showing they weren't limited by the beliefs about their gender and could compete at the highest levels of sports.

And, because women's preferences and equipment needs differed, there was a need to focus on female centric designs that were not only functional and supportive but attractive enough that women would enjoy wearing them. Athleisure became fashionable because fitness and sports had become a part of women's lives, and once these athletes finally had stylish options to wear that they didn't feel embarrassed to be seen in public wearing, their gym clothes became part of their casual wardrobe.

**

Athleisure is easy to define, until you realize that history has seen this story before and athleisure is just the latest chapter of activewear turned casual clothes. Sportswear began as athletic clothes used for sports and became fashionable every day clothes through the influence of designers and then hip hop culture.

The popularity of athleisure, or workout clothes worn for exercise and casually, led to an increase in the number of brands offering athletic clothing and footwear options. However, the shift in focus of athletic clothing from technical to fashion is not well received by those connected to top athletic brands. Some of them believe the term has come to imply laziness while fashion-focused brands believe the term doesn't adequately capture the element of style.

However, there is room for both technical and fashionable athletic clothing to co-exist. And, for lack of a better term, the word athleisure currently remains a way to describe when fashionable athletic clothing is worn casually...or simply, the way more of us dress today.

**

Athleisure is brand driven is false because women and their communities are the driving the movement. As more women participated in sports there was a new generation of women who grew up active and had a desire to continue fitness into adulthood. This created the perfect storm of athleisure influencing the rise of fitness and conversely, fitness influencing the rise of athleisure.

And more than fitness classes, women have taken their communities online, influencing and motivating each other through social media and blogs as well as providing feedback to brands about their products.

Women, especially young women, are now part of the two-way conversation with brands in two ways, first with their purchases and second with their direct feedback and ability to share what they like and dislike with each other that can help a brand grow or leave it behind. Most importantly, women now have a platform they can use to not only respond but impart even more change through voicing what they want.

**

One size fits all is one of the biggest falsehoods of all. Despite how far women's athletic clothing has come, there is still a ways to go. The average U.S. woman is around a size 16 but most activewear and athleisure options are made for women between 0 and 14. That just doesn't make sense.

Women come in all shapes and sizes and all women are athletes (*remember, if you have a body, you are an athlete*), therefore we need more size options that accommodate more women beyond standard sizes. Working out should not be limited to women of a certain shape and size.

Long held beliefs about what a fit woman should look like need to be retired. Athletes build muscle in different ways, so instead of judging women for how they look, they should be praised for their strength and athleticism. Whether using their voice to speak out or starting their own brands to provide more options, women are changing the narrative and brands are beginning to respond with inclusive sizes and options for all athletes.

**

Leggings aren't pants is my favorite falsehood. Let me repeat this, leggings cover a women's legs and so therefore are pants. Regardless, the debate over whether leggings are pants is the wrong one.

It's not as if women haven't been wearing leggings for decades. The difference today is that athleisure leggings are thinner than casual options in the past, showing the outline of a women's body more closely and creating an awkward situation if they are ill-fitting and become see-through. So, the debate should actually focus on whether women's leggings fit correctly.

In addition to fit, the appropriateness of leggings is also up for debate; however, in the 1920s it was considered scandalous for women to show their ankles in public, so it's really only a matter of time before leggings become as common for women to wear with tops of any length as jeans or any other pant.

**

Athleisure is lazy dismisses the reality that going to the gym isn't the only way to maintain an active lifestyle. Women are busy and are increasingly creating a fitness-focused lifestyle in whatever way they can, be that working out at home, heading to the gym, being a tourist in a new city, or heading outside for a hike. Each option lends itself to different technical, design, and fashion preferences.

For the modern woman, wearing athleisure during the day gives her the flexibility to move more than she would have otherwise, whether that means taking the stairs, going for an impromptu walk, or heading to a fitness class with a friend after work. Women want clothes that are comfortable, functional, and stylish so they can focus on their day rather than how their clothes fit.

**

"Shrink it and pink it" works is one of the most important falsehoods. The approach to shrink and pink men's styles for women assumes that all women like pink and want to look like little men. This would be hilarious if it wasn't so infuriating.

Women's athletic apparel and footwear should not be considered an afterthought. Women are half the population and deserve the level of effort and attention required to suit the needs of such a large group. After being virtually neglected for many years, women's sportswear and athletic apparel are finally receiving more focus and resources.

The rise in athletic clothing sales is happening because women now have more options. And it's not all about women's only products; sometimes women want the same style as offered to men but in their size.

Brands need to be tapped into what women want and whether that is the same or a different style (or both). Instead of assuming what women want, brands need to simply ask and respond. Most importantly, it's necessary that women are involved in the strategy, design, and marketing to make sure women's needs are met.

**

Men should design women's clothing speaks to the falsehood that persists in the apparel industry where men are making the decisions for women's clothes. Why are people that never wear the clothes designing it? That just doesn't make sense to me. Men tend to design clothes for women that they think women look beautiful in versus female designers that create options that are both beautiful and functional for their lives.

Some women are meeting this challenge head-on by starting their own activewear brands with designs they want to wear but couldn't find to purchase. These female-led brands are not only giving women more female-focused options but are also providing more leadership opportunities for women. Though, regardless of company size, more women are needed in leadership positions at all brands that offer women's apparel to ensure that women's needs are being met.

Athleisure is sustainable is not exactly true for clothing made with polyester or other synthetic fibers. The reason why activewear and athleisure has awesome properties like moisture-wicking, compression, and more is because it's made with polyester. The downside of that fabric is it is made with chemicals that aren't sustainable. The increased manufacturing and use of clothing with this material puts a strain on the environment in both making and disposing of them in landfills because they will not decompose like clothes made with natural fabric.

Brands are responding in various ways to provide more sustainable options, from using recycled materials to encouraging fewer purchases and longer use through providing repair services or resale programs. Unfortunately, recent discoveries about micro-fibers have found that these tiny fibers break off your clothes when you wash them and find their way through the water system, polluting the oceans. These challenges will need to be resolved and supported by more brands and consumers.

**

Athleisure has limited influence speaks to the falsehood that athleisure's popularity is limited to sports related clothing. Athleisure has changed what women want and expect from their clothing. When leggings sales went up, jean's sales declined until more stretch was incorporated into jeans to add comfort. Similarly, more clothing beyond athletic is being made with technical fabrics and properties once reserved for sport.

As women lead more active lives and demand comfortable clothes, more clothes will be made with fabrics that are versatile and easy to care for but in classic styles and silhouettes typically worn to the office or other events. And the comfort of athleisure extends to undergarments. Younger women are not responding to the need to meet a fantasy ideal that is uncomfortable, they want their lingerie to fit and move with them in the same natural way as their other clothes, responding to brands that speak to these needs with authenticity.

**

So, now that we got through all of that, how will athleisure and athletic inspired clothing continue to evolve?

[Raises hand] I've got a few theories.

Several factors are at play – sports participation, generational shifts, women's movements, and technology. Sports breed leadership, so as more young women participate in sports, the greater the chances of even more female leadership in the future. More female voices in leadership roles will have several implications for clothing. As we've already seen, female focused clothes are more functional, inclusive, and versatile without sacrificing style.

Driving a lot of the shift towards athleisure are younger generations, Millennials and Gen Z. As you've seen, I'm just one of many women choosing clothes that are versatile and comfortable. Wearing clothes that allow you to move and feel good is addicting.

This will only continue to grow. I expect a lot more pockets and more easily managed zipper locations in women's futures, in addition to clothes that can be worn in many ways. Fewer clothes, but better and more adaptable.

More than older generations these women are making their voices heard and impacting the success of brands at scale. Their preference for wearing practical and comfortable clothes has pushed the definitions of acceptable clothes in several environments from schools to work. Like generations before them, these women are not allowing rules to dictate their clothing decisions.

Female leaders who prefer more practical clothing will eventually move from pushing the definition of appropriate attire to defining it as they move into leadership positions and become a greater percentage of the workforce. Athleisure and more comfortable clothing will not only become more common place, but it will also continue to influence the way other clothes are designed and made, from adding elements that make the clothes more comfortable to leveraging the same material as athleisure for dress shirts and more formal clothing.

The functionality of clothes will increase in importance. Clothes aren't just about looking pretty anymore, they need to perform to the level that women need them to. Whether that's being washable, helping an athlete run a marathon, or provide comfort throughout a long work day, more women want and are responding to options that help them navigate a crazy schedule and feel good to wear.

Above all, more options will continue to be created for women of all shapes and sizes. Through social media and their buying power as customers and through leadership and entrepreneurial ventures, women are demanding more inclusivity and authentic acceptance of women as they are instead of promoting unrealistic images and standards.

As women take more control over the direction and design of clothing, the message will be less focused on how the clothes make women more attractive and more about how they make women feel while wearing them. A female-run, female-focused, and female-designed world will not be led with a "sex sells" approach.

What started out as women simply deciding to wear yoga pants to brunch has snowballed into a powerful movement where women's voices and actions are changing the power dynamic toward the voice of the female customer and entrepreneur.

Out with assumptions about what women want and are told they look good wearing, and in with female-led and female-focused designs and messaging. Women aren't as open to being told what to wear anymore; they'd rather tell you what they'd like to wear. And, in the future women won't just be voicing their opinions, they will be leading and making key decisions about how clothes are designed in leadership roles. It's only a matter of time.

Athleisure helped ignite a fashion movement, and it's *just* beginning.

ACKNOWLEDGEMENTS

This book has been a wonderful journey. What started years ago as a frustration grew into curiosity and eventually developed into a full-blown passion for something not everyone understood but so many supported.

First and foremost, I could not have completed this book without the patience of my insanely supportive friends and family. Thank you for answering the phone when you knew I was calling to talk about this book yet *again*, reading early chapters, and providing your honest feedback. I am fortunate to have so many caring people in my life.

I also could not have completed this book without the women and men who were willing to speak with me about their thoughts on athletic clothing and personal experiences.

I was blessed to have been able to speak with athletes, entrepreneurs, industry leaders, and consultants who not only provided me with their insight, but also connected me with others to speak to. Thank you all.

And last but certainly not least, I'd like to thank my publisher, New Degree Press. To Eric Koester and Brian Bies, thank you for believing in the idea of this book as much as I did and your guidance throughout the process.

REFERENCES CITED

INTRODUCTION

"Is Activewear Industry Finally Becoming Overstretched?", October 10, 2016. *PYMNTS.Com.*

Hanbury, Mary. "A Dominant American Clothing Style is Back from the Dead — But Athleisure Has Changed It Forever". *Business Insider,* April 3, 2018.

Kell, John. "A Bunch of New Brands are Joining the Athleisure Wear Craze". *Fortune*, October 22, 2016.

FALSEHOOD 1

Chang, Mahalia. "Style Revolution: 10 Feminist Fashion Trends that Changed the World". *ELLE*, May 13, 2018.

Chung, Madelyn. "Victoria Beckham Says She 'Can't Do' Heels Anymore, At Least At Work". *Huffpost Canada*, February 26, 2016.

Collins, Lauren. "Sole Mate: Christian Louboutin and the Psychology of Shoes.". *The New Yorker*, March 28, 2011.

Cunningham, Patricia A. *Reforming Women's Fashion, 1850-1920*. Kent State Univ Press, 2003.

Donovan, Carrie. "Feminism's Effect on Fashion". *The New York Times*, August 28, 1977.

Ell, Kellie. "Sneaker Sales are Growing as Sales of High Heels Tumble". *CNBC*, May 20, 2018.

"The Gender Bending History of the High Heel". Podcast. *99% Invisible*. June 14, 2014.

Hyland, Véronique. "When Sweatpants Become a Form of Protest". *The CUT,* October 28, 2014.

Johnson, Adela. "Hell for High Heels". *Footwearplusmagazine.Com*, July 1, 2018.

Komar, Marlen. "How Women Have Used Fashion as a Feminist Tool". *Bustle*, November 17, 2016.

U.S. Department of Labor Blog. 12 Stats About Working Women | U.S. Department of Labor Blog. March 1, 2017.

FALSEHOOD 2

The Denver Post. "Americans are Running Marathons Slower Than Ever, A New Report Says. But Why?", July 17, 2017.

Given, Karen. From the 'Jockbra' to Brandi Chastain: The History of the Sports Bra. Lisa Lindahl Interview by Radio. WBUR 90.9 Boston. February 24, 2017.

Karlstrom, Solvie. "Sweaty Betty Founder Tamara Hill-Norton on Reshaping an Industry – And your Bum". Blog. *The Thread | Nordstrom Fashion Blog & Fashion Week Updates*. April 4, 2018.

Kansara, Vikram Alexei. "Tamara Hill-Norton of Sweaty Betty on Seizing the Opportunity in Activewear". *Business of Fashion*, April 10, 2014.

Lee, Jaeah, and Maya Dusenbery. "Charts: The State of Women's Athletics, 40 Years After Title IX". *Mother Jones*, June 22, 2012.

Lindahl, Lisa. "About". *Lisalindahl.Com*, Accessed October 30, 2018.

Mink, Michael. "Chip Wilson's Design Made Lululemon a Winner". *Investor's Business Daily*, June 8, 2012.

Olmstead, Maegan. "Title IX and The Rise of Female Athletes in America – Women's Sports Foundation". *Women's Sports Foundation*, September 2, 2016.

Pasquarelli, Adrianne. "Activewear Makes it onto the Runway", *Crain's New York Business*. July 10, 2011.

Price, Susan. "Sweaty Betty is Betting American Women Will Fall for its Workout Wear with a London Vibe", *Forbes*, November 21, 2016.

Raz, Guy. "Lululemon Athletica: Chip Wilson". Podcast. *How I Built This with Guy Raz*. June 18, 2018.

Roberts, Daniel. "Athleisure is Still Driving Clothing Sales". *Yahoo Finance*, November 24, 2017.

Sherman, Lauren. "Sorry, But Athleisure is Not Dead". *The Business of Fashion,* May 3, 2018.

Warner, Fara. "GRASS-ROOTS BUSINESS; Dressing Women to Sweat, Fashionably". *The New York Times,* July. 6, 2003.

FALSEHOOD 3

"Athletic Lifestyles Keep Apparel Sales Healthy". *Morgan Stanley,* October 30, 2015.

Clark, Evan. "Christine Day on Her adidas Gig and Why Ath-Leisure's a Bad Word". *WWD,* February 22, 2016.

"History". *adidas,* Accessed October 20, 2018.

Mellery-Pratt, Robin. "Why are Sportswear Giants Nike and adidas Embracing Fashion?". *The Business of Fashion,* October 21, 2015.

The NPD Group, Inc. "U.S. Athletic Footwear Industry Sales Grew 2 Percent to $19.6 Billion in 2017, NPD Group Reports", February 6, 2018.

Segran, Elizabeth. "adidas Makes a Play for Women". *Fast Company,* February 6, 2016a.

Segran, Elizabeth. "Bandier Would Like Us to Retire the Word "Athleisure"". *Fast Company*, September 12, 2016b.

Shackleton, Holly. "There Are No Rules: How Yohji Yamamoto is Taking Y-3 to the Next Level". *i-D*, June 1, 2016.

Spagnolo, Angelo. "Walking Backwards into the Future: Analyzing 15 Years of Y-3". *Grailed*, February 19, 2018.

Studeman, Kristin Tice. "From Alexander Wang to Beyonce, Everyone's Doing It: A Look at How Gym-To-Street Became the New Uniform". *Vogue*, October 28, 2014.

Trefis Team. "The Athleisure Trend is Here to Stay", *Forbes*, October 6, 2016.

Wilson, Chip. "Why the Word "Athleisure" is Completely Misunderstood". *Forbes*, April 18, 2018.

FALSEHOOD 4

Aslam, Salman. "Instagram By the Numbers (2018): Stats, Demographics & Fun Facts". *Omnicore*. Accessed October 30, 2018a.

Aslam, Salman. "Pinterest By the Numbers (2018): Stats, Demographics & Fun Facts". *Omnicore*. Accessed October 30, 2018b.

Chaffee, Ian. "Forget About Sexism: Now TV Coverage of Women's Sports is Just Plain Boring". *USC News*, September 12, 2017.

Dogtiev, Artyom. "Facebook Revenue and Usage Statistics (2018)". *Business of Apps*. Accessed October 30, 2018.

Forbes. "The World's Highest-Paid Athletes", 2018.

"Global Twitter User Distribution as of October 2018, By Gender". *Statista*. Accessed November 28, 2018.

Iqbal, Mansoor. "Snapchat Revenue and Usage Statistics (2018)". *Business of Apps*. Accessed October 30, 2018.

Mau, Dhani. "The Rise Of 'Instagram Brands': How the Platform is Leveling the Fashion Playing Field". *Fashionista*, May 2, 2018.

"Millennial Women Have Strong Purchasing Power. What Influences It? – Marketing Charts". *Marketing Charts*, March 19, 2018.

Trefis Team. "The Athleisure Trend is Here to Stay", *Forbes*, October 6, 2016.

"Twitter: Number of Monthly Active U.S. Users 2010-2018". *Statista*. Accessed October 30, 2018.

Weiss, Richard. "adidas Hires Social-Media Stars to Double Women's Market Share". *Bloomberg*, March 14, 2017.

"Women are Driving the Social Media Revolution". *Connectamericas*. Accessed November 25, 2018.

"Women in Sport". *International Olympic Committee*. Accessed December 1, 2018.

FALSEHOOD 5

Barsamian, Edward. "Serena Williams Shares Her On-Court Style Secret and What She's Looking Forward to This Fall". *Vogue*, August 29, 2016.

Christel, Deborah A., Nicole H. O'Donnell, and Linda Arthur Bradley. 2016. "Coping by Crossdressing: An Exploration of Exercise Clothing for Obese Heterosexual Women". *Fashion and Textiles* 3 (1). doi:10.1186/s40691-016-0063-z.

The Economist. "The Forgotten Majority: The Fashion Industry Pays Attention to Plus-Size Women", July 13, 2017.

Ewen, Lara. "Why Plus-Size Fashion Is Still Struggling With Image Problems". *Retail Dive*, May 31, 2016.

Global News. *Lululemon Yoga Pants Uproar*. Video. November 8, 2013.

Huffington Post. "Chip Wilson Lululemon Pants Comments Spark Social Outrage (TWEETS)", November 7, 2013.

Humphrey, Michael. "A Chat with Cassey Ho: On Target, Thigh Gaps and Health-Body Balance". *Forbes*, April 17, 2014.

Nittle, Nadra. "Plus-Size Activewear Shouldn't Be So Hard to Find". *Racked*, July 10, 2018.

Rabimov, Stephan. "Universal Standard Gets a Plus on Size and Style". *Forbes*, October 18, 2017.

Reebok. "Reebok Releases First of its Kind Sports Bra Featuring New Reactive Technology", August 6, 2018.

Rinkunas, Susan. "Serena Williams Does Not Deign to Wrestle with Sweat-Soaked Sports Bras". *The CUT*, August 26, 2016.

Wilde, Kristin. "Women in Sport: Gender Stereotypes in the Past and Present". Undergraduate, Athabasca University. 2007.

Williams, Serena. "Letter to My Mom". *Reddit.Com,* 2017.

Young, Sarah. "Nike Finally Launches Its First Plus-Size Range". *The Independent*, March 3, 2017.

FALSEHOOD 6

Dockterman, Eliana. "When Enforcing School Dress Codes Turns into Slut Shaming". *TIME*, March 25, 2014.

Harrington, Rebecca, and Benjamin Zhang. "People Are Freaking Out That United Told Women They Couldn't Wear Leggings on a Flight — Here's What Really Happened". *Yahoo!*, March 26, 2017.

Koo-Seen-Lin, Nina. "The History of Hemlines". *Women's History Network*, September 1, 2013.

Lee, Yhe-Young. "Controversies About American Women's Fashion, 1920-1945: Through the Lens of The New York Times". Retrospective Theses and Dissertations, Iowa State University, 2013.

Malinsky, Rebecca, and Katharine K. Zarrella. "Once and for All: Are Leggings Pants?". *The Wall Street Journal*, July 3, 2018.

Nahman, Haley. "America Hates Denim, Loves Leggings: The Proof is in the Data/Our Hearts". Blog. *Man Repeller*. October 27, 2016.

Ritzen, Stacey. "This Woman's Rant on Why 'Leggings Aren't Pants' Is Breaking the Damn Internet". *UPROXX*, October 26, 2015.

FALSEHOOD 7

"2018 Employee Benefits: The Evolution of Benefits". Society for Human Resource Management, 2018.

Agins, Teri. *The End of Fashion*. New York: HarperCollins World. 2001.

"Carbon38's Katie Warner Johnson on the Deeper Significance of Athleisure". Blog. *The Daily Front Row*, July 13, 2018.

Halzack, Sarah. "A Chart About Leggings Sales That Should Scare Every Old-School Apparel Chain". *The Washington Post*, October 19, 2016.

The NPD Group, Inc. "The Casualization of American Apparel: Will the Athleisure Trend Stay or Go?", August 20, 2018.

Salemi, Vicki. "If You Want Productive Employees, Let Them Wear Sweatpants". *New York Post*, April 4, 2016.

FALSEHOOD 8

Abel, Katie. "How Silicon Valley Darling Allbirds Became A Footwear Phenomenon". *Yahoo!*, April 30, 2018.

Bain, Marc. "Under Armour Is Learning the Hard Way That Sportswear is as Much About Fashion As Performance". *Quartz*, January 31, 2017.

Baskin, Anna. "Is Homegating The New Tailgating?". *Adage*, September 21, 2011.

BMO Financial Group. "Financial Concerns of Women". BMO Wealth Institute Report US Edition. 2015.

Bobila, Maria. "Female Fans Voice What's Wrong with the Sneaker Industry". *Fashionista*, July 17, 2015.

Bobila, Maria. "A Team Of 14 Female Nike Designers Were Tasked with Reimagining the Air Force 1 and Air Jordan 1". *Fashionista*, January 18, 2018.

Bruzas, Ashley. "Sneakers for Women are Finally Improving". *Highsnobiety*, October 8, 2018.

Contrera, Jessica. "The End Of 'Shrink It and Pink It': A History of Advertisers Missing the Mark with Women". *The Washington Post*, June 8, 2016.

Findling, Deborah. "Allbirds, The Sustainable Sneaker That's Growing in Popularity Without A Big Brand Name". *CNBC*, January 1, 2017.

Gray, Alistair. "Under Armour breaks from 'athleisure' craze". *Financial Times*, December 26, 2018.

Harwell, Drew. "Women Are One of The Sporting-Goods Industry's Biggest-Growing Markets — And One of Its Most Ignored". *Washington Post*, October 14, 2014.

King, Michelle. "Want A Piece of the 18 Trillion Dollar Female Economy? Start with Gender Bias". *Forbes*, May 24, 2017.

Kish, Matthew. "Former Lululemon CEO Christine Day to Help adidas Boost Its Women's Sector". *Bizwomen*, February 17, 2016.

Malinsky, Becky. "Stella Mccartney On How to Look Good When You Work Out (With Her Newest adidas Collection, Of Course)". *Glamour*, May 7, 2013.

McCarthy, Michael. "Ad of The Day: Ballerina Misty Copeland Stars In Jaw-Dropping Spot For Under Armour". *Adweek*, August 1, 2014.

Palmieri, Jean E. "Under Armour Seeks to Explode Women's Business". *WWD*, July 31, 2014.

Schneider-Levy, Barbara, and Katie Abel. "Allbirds Has Sold A Million Pairs of Shoes in Two Years & Is Launching A New Collection Made From Trees". *Footwear News*, March 15, 2018.

Schultz, E.J.. "Ad Age's 2014 Marketer of the Year: Under Armour". *Ad Age*, December 8, 2014.

Thomas, Lauren. "Allbirds Is Opening a Massive Store In New York and Plans More Across the US". *CNBC*, September 4, 2018.

Under Armour. "Under Armour And Misty Copeland Launch the Misty Copeland Signature Collection, Celebrating Strength and Style", May 3, 2018.

Wilson, Mark. "How Pink and Blue Became Gender-Specific". *Fast Company,* June 6, 2013.

FALSEHOOD 9

Allen, Lisa. "How Lorna Jane Clarkson Took on the Activewear World". *The Australian Business Review,* June 19, 2015.

The CEO Magazine. "Meet the judges: Lorna Jane Clarkson, Founder and CCO of Lorna Jane". June 1, 2018.

Caplan-Bricker, Nora. "Ty Haney is the Queen of Athleisure". *Outside Online*, June 5, 2018.

Dunn, Emily. "Women in Business Q&A: Katie Warner Johnson, Founder And CEO, Carbon38". *Huffington Post*, December 31, 2017a.

Dunn, Emily. "Women in Business Q&A: Nancy Green, President And CEO, Athleta". *Huffington Post*, October 2, 2017b.

EY and espnW. "Where Will You Find Your Next Leader?". EYGM Limited. 2015.

Koltun, Natalie. "Athleta Bucks 'Girls in Sports' Stereotypes with Back-to-School Push". *Marketing Dive*. August 6, 2018.

Lieber, Chavie. "Athleta Doesn't Ignore Older Women and That's Why It's Successful". *Racked*, September 14, 2017.

"Lorna Jane Clarkson ★ Chief Creative Office + Founder / Lorna Jane Active Wear". 2018. *The Cool Career*. Accessed October 25.

Marikar, Sheila. "How This Ballerina Became A $20 Million Business Owner". *Inc.*, July/August 2016.

Miller, Claire Cain, Kevin Quealy, and Margot Sanger-Katz. "The Top Jobs Where Women Are Outnumbered By Men Named John". *The New York Times*, April 24, 2018.

Pesce, Nicole Lyn. "One Mom's Viral Twitter Thread Renews Women's Calls for Pockets". *Moneyish*, April 24, 2018.

Sherlock, Rachel. "Lorna Jane, The Australian Entrepreneur who Created Activewear". *CrowdInk*, September 5, 2017.

Sullivan, Robert. "How Outdoor Voices Is Taking Over the Fitness-Apparel World". *Vogue*, January 11, 2018.

Thomas, Lauren. "Athletic Apparel Start-Up Outdoor Voices Raises $34 Million In Latest Round of Funding". *CNBC*, March 13, 2018.

Warner, Fara. "Grass-Roots Business; Dressing Women to Sweat, Fashionably". *The New York Times*, July 6, 2003.

FALSEHOOD 10

"Athletic Footwear Chases Fast Fashion". *Morgan Stanley,* July 5, 2017.

"Athletic Lifestyles Keep Apparel Sales Healthy". *Morgan Stanley,* October 30, 2015.

Boucher, J., and D. Friot. "Primary Microplastics in the Oceans: A Global Evaluation of Sources". *IUCN Publication.* 2017. doi:10.2305/iucn.ch.2017.01.en.

"Create Employee Champions and Customer Advocates Around Your Mission". *B the Change,* May 31, 2018.

Cunningham, Erin. "Stella McCartney Is Making the Best Damn Athleisure Out There". *Refinery29,* November 7, 2016.

Farra, Emily. "adidas By Stella McCartney". *Vogue,* February 1, 2018.

Hoguet, Deidre. "Sustainability and Performance in Textiles: Can You Have It All?". *The Guardian,* April 10, 2014.

Leighton, Mara. "The Internet Can't Stop Talking About These Leggings Made of Recycled Water Bottles — And Now I Understand Why". *Business Insider,* July 23, 2018.

Nicholson, Sibel. "adidas Sold 1 Million Eco-Friendly Shoes Made of Ocean Plastic In 2017". *Interesting Engineering,* March 16, 2018.

NIKE, Inc. "FY16/17 Sustainable Business Report NIKE, Inc.", 2018.

"Recycled Poly | Prana". *Prana.Com,* Accessed November 25, 2018.

Remy, Nathalie, Eveline Speelman, and Steven Swartz. "Style That's Sustainable: A New Fast-Fashion Formula". *McKinsey & Company*, Accessed November 25, 2018.

Saner, Emine. "Sustainable Style: Will Gen Z Help the Fashion Industry Clean Up Its Act?". *The Guardian*, April 25, 2017.

The Story of Stuff Project. *The Story of Microfibers*. Video. Accessed November 25, 2018.

FALSEHOOD 11

"5 Retail Trends to Watch". *Synchrony Financial News*, July 2016.

Bhasin, Kim. "How Blue Jeans are Mounting a Comeback in a Yoga Pants World". *The Chicago Tribune*, April 2, 2018.

Bhattarai, Abha. "$350 Jeans Are Dead. $100 Leggings Killed Them.". *The Washington Post*, July 7, 2017.

Brassil, Gillian. "L Brands Tumbles After Weak Sales At 'Broken' Brand Victoria's Secret". *CNBC*, July 12, 2018.

"Denim's Demise: How Athletic Wear is Impacting the Jean Business". August 10, 2016. *PYMNTS.Com*.

Harper, Leah. "The Victoria's Secret Backlash: How Athleisure-Inspired Bras Have Seen Off the Sexy Look". *The Guardian*, November 9, 2018.

Howland, Daphne. "American Eagle Sees 'Tremendous Opportunity' In Aerie". *Retail Dive*, March 12, 2018.

"Levi's® Iconic 501® Jeans Gets The Stretch Treatment". *Levi Strauss*, September 20, 2016.

The NPD Group, Inc. "Millennials Have Triggered an Evolution in the Way Women Shop for Bras, Reports NPD", February 22, 2016.

O'Connor, Tamison. "As Athleisure Cools, Denim Heats Up". *Business of Fashion*, November 17, 2017.

Roberts, Daniel. "Athleisure Is Still Driving Clothing Sales". *Yahoo Finance*, November 24, 2017.

Made in the USA
Monee, IL
01 December 2019

17757055R00154